Algebra

Table of Contents

Kelley Wingate Publications
An imprint of Carson-Dellosa Publishing LLC
PO Box 35665 • Greensboro, NC 27425 USA

© 2009, Carson-Dellosa Publishing LLC. The purchase of this material entitles the buyer to reproduce worksheets and activities for classroom use only—not for commercial resale. Reproduction of these materials for an entire school or district is prohibited. No part of this book may be reproduced (except as noted above), stored in a retrieval system, or transmitted in any form or by any means (mechanically, electronically, recording, etc.) without the prior written consent of Carson-Dellosa Publishing LLC. Kelley Wingate Publications is an imprint of Carson-Dellosa Publishing LLC.

Printed in the USA • All rights reserved.
Revised Edition 2010

ISBN 078-1-60418-266-8

How to Use This Book

This book was designed to help students practice and master mathematics skills. The stronger their foundation is, the easier it will be for them to move into higher levels of mathematics.

The activities in this book cover such topics as variables and equations, polynomials, factoring, and graphing. The pages may be used as supplemental material, or as enrichment for any algebra program. After completing the pages in this book, students will be adequately prepared for the study of geometry and pre-calculus.

All students learn at their own rate; therefore, use your judgment to introduce concepts when it is developmentally appropriate.

Hands-On Learning

Hands-on learning reinforces the skills covered within the activity pages and improves students' potential for understanding. The flash cards at the back of this book may be utilized for basic skill and enrichment activities. Pull out the flash cards and cut them apart. Use the flash cards as practice and reinforcement of basic algebraic concepts.

Resources

Solving Equations

Whenever you are faced with the situation of solving an equation (whether it is simple or complicated), always remember, *if the variable is alone on one side of the equation sign, the answer will also be alone on the other side.*

To put it simply, Variable = Answer.

Use the following steps to help you solve equations.

1. Simplify parentheses using the distributive property.

2. Combine like terms independently on each side of the equation.

3. Move all variables to the left side of the equation by using addition and subtraction.

4. Move all numbers to the right side of the equation using addition and subtraction.

5. Simplify with multiplication and division.

Exponents

$x^2 = x \cdot x$	x is the base; 2 is the exponent.
$x^a \cdot x^b = x^{a+b}$	If you have the <u>same</u> base, add the exponents.
$(x^a)^b = x^{a \times b}$	If you raise a power to a power, multiply exponents.
$\dfrac{x^a}{x^b} = x^{a \times b}$	If you divide with the same base, subtract exponents.
$x^{-a} = \dfrac{1}{x^a}$	Negative exponents mean that you must take the reciprocal of the expression.
$(xy)^a = x^a y^a$	All terms in parentheses share the exponent.

CD-104316 • © Carson-Dellosa

How to Use This Book

Factoring $x^2 + bx + c$

To factor an expression, use the following methods as they are ordered.

1. GCF: Greatest Common Factor

> Example: $6x + 6y = 6(x + y)$
> Example: $2x^2 + 4x = 2x(x + 2)$

2. DOTS: Difference of Two Squares

> $a^2 - b^2 = (a + b)(a - b)$
> Example: $3x^2 - 27 = 3(x^2 - 9) = 3(x + 3)(x - 3)$
> Example: $x^2 - 121 = (x + 11)(x - 11)$

3. FOIL: First Outer Inner Last

Let the addition and subtraction signs guide your factoring.
First, in your problem, look at the second sign.
  If the second sign is positive, use same signs in factors.
  If the second sign is negative, use different signs in factors.
Second, look at the first sign in your problem.

If the second sign is positive—

If the first sign is positive, both signs in factoring will be positive.
Example:

   $x^2 + 7x + 10$ (second sign positive)
   $x^2 + 7x + 10$ (first sign positive)
   $(x + 2)(x + 5)$ (both signs positive)

If the first sign is negative, both signs in factoring will be negative.
Example:

   $x^2 - 7x + 10$ (second sign positive)
   $x^2 - 7x + 10$ (first sign negative)
   $(x - 2)(x - 5)$ (both signs negative)

If the second sign is negative—

If the first sign is negative, the sign of the larger factor will be negative.
Example:

   $x^2 - 3x - 10$ (second sign negative)
   $x^2 - 3x + 10$ (first sign negative)
   $(x - 5)(x + 2)$ (larger factor negative)

If the first sign is positive, the sign of the larger factor will be positive.
Example:

   $x^2 + 3x - 10$ (second sign negative)
   $x^2 + 3x - 10$ (first sign positive)
   $(x + 5)(x - 2)$ (larger factor positive)

Operations with Real Numbers

Operations with Real Numbers

Integers are . . . $^-5, ^-4, ^-3, ^-2, ^-1, 0, 1, 2, 3, 4, 5 . . .$
There is a set of three dots before and after the list of integers. This means that the numbers continue, and there is no largest or smallest integer.

Looking at a number line, the integers to the right of zero are **positive integers** and the integers to the left of zero are **negative integers**. Zero is neither a positive integer nor a negative integer.

Natural numbers are all positive integers.
    1, 2, 3, 4, 5 . . .

Whole numbers are comprised of zero and all of the positive integers.
    0, 1, 2, 3, 4, 5 . . .

Variables are letters of the alphabet that represent a number in mathematics. For example, in the problem $5x = 15$, x is the variable.

The quotient of two integers is a **rational number**. A rational number can be written as $\frac{t}{x}$, in the case that t and x are integers and x is not equal to zero ($x \neq 0$). When a rational number is written this way, it is called a **fraction**.

It is important to note that every integer is a rational number. A decimal number, such as 12.6, is also considered a rational number. All rational numbers can be written as repeating or terminating decimals.

An **irrational number** is a number whose decimal expansion does not terminate and never repeats. For example $\pi = 3.141592604 . . .$

Real numbers are made up of rational numbers and irrational numbers.

CD-104316 • © Carson-Dellosa

Name _____   Date _____

Operations with Real Numbers

Patterns

The French mathematician Blaise Pascal developed a triangular pattern to describe the coefficients for the expansion of $(a + b)^n$, for consecutive values of n in rows. This pattern is referred to as Pascal's triangle.

In the triangular formation below, note that $(a + b)^0 = 1$ and $(a + b)^1 = a + b$.

Part A. Fill in the blanks in Pascal's triangle to extend the pattern.

$n = 0$ 1

$n = 1$ 1   1

$n = 2$ 1   2   1

$n = 3$ 1   3   3   1

$n = 4$ 1   ____   6   ____   ____

$n = 5$ ____ ____ ____ 10 ____ ____

$n = 6$ ____ ____ ____ ____ ____ ____ ____

$n = 7$ ____ ____ ____ ____ ____ ____ ____ ____

$n = 8$ ____ ____ ____ ____ ____ ____ ____ ____ ____

$n = 9$ ____ ____ ____ ____ ____ ____ ____ ____ ____ ____

$n = 10$ ____ ____ ____ ____ ____ ____ ____ ____ ____ ____ ____

Part B. Use Pascal's triangle to find the coefficients of the expansion $(a + b)$.

1. $(a + b)^3 = $ ____$a^3 + $ ____$a^2b + $ ____$ab^2 + $ ____b^3

2. $(a + b)^6 = $ ____$a^6 + $ ____$a^5b + $ ____$a^4b^2 + $ ____$a^3b^3 + $ ____$a^2b^4 + $ ____$ab^5 + $ ____b^6

3. $(a + b)^4 = $ ____$a^4 + $ ____$a^3b + $ ____$a^2b^2 + $ ____$ab^3 + $ ____b^4

4. $(a + b)^7 = $ ____$a^7 + $ ____$a^6b + $ ____$a^5b^2 + $ ____$a^4b^3 + $ ____$a^3b^4 + $ ____$a^2b^5 + $ ____$ab^6 + $ ____b^7

Operations with Real Numbers

Patterns

Carefully study the patterns of numbers to complete each pattern.

1. 130, 120, 110, 100, _____, _____, _____, _____

2. 20, 200, 2,000, 20,000, _____, _____, _____

3. 3, 6, 7, 14, 15, 30, 31, _____, _____, _____, _____

4. 1, 4, 9, 16, 25, _____, _____, _____, _____, _____

5. 1, 6, 5, 10, 9, 14, 13, _____, _____, _____, _____

6. $\frac{1}{2}, \frac{2}{3}, \frac{3}{4}, \frac{4}{5}, \frac{5}{6}, \frac{6}{7},$ _____, _____, _____, _____

7. 17, 15, 25, 23, 33, 31, _____, _____, _____, _____

8. 7, 21, 63, 189, _____, _____, _____, _____

9. 800, 80, 8, 0.8, 0.08, _____, _____, _____, _____

Challenge! The following is a special pattern called the Fibonacci sequence. **See if you can discover and complete this interesting pattern.**

1, 1, 2, 3, 5, 8, 13, _____, _____, _____, _____, _____

                                                                                 CD-104316 • © Carson-Dellosa

Name _____   Date _____

Operations with Real Numbers

Adding Real Numbers

$$^-7 + 6 = {}^-1$$

Add.

1. $2.7 + (^-4.8) =$

2. $1.45 + 2.65 + (^-9.43) =$

3. $^-55 + (^-8) + (^-4) + 54 =$

4. $3.54 + 4.27 + 7.43 =$

5. $10 + 7 + (^-7) + (^-10) =$

6. $16 + 21 + (^-3) + 7 =$

7. $10 + 7 + (^-16) + 9 + (^-30) =$

8. $5.8 + 8.4 =$

9. $2.76 + (^-6.56) + (^-9.72) =$

10. $8 + (^-7) =$

11. $2\frac{3}{5} + 4\frac{3}{7} =$

12. $^-8\frac{3}{5} + 3\frac{3}{7} =$

13. $3\frac{5}{8} + (^-1\frac{2}{3}) + 2 =$

14. $^-5\frac{3}{4} + (^-2\frac{3}{4}) + 8 =$

15. $7.3 + (3.9) =$

16. $^-21 + 12 + (^-1) + (^-17) =$

17. $7.867 + (^-5.329) =$

18. $^-2\frac{3}{5} + (^-5\frac{3}{7}) + 3 =$

19. $3 + 12 + (^-13) + 36 =$

20. $^-3\frac{1}{6} + (^-9\frac{3}{12}) + 6 =$

Operations with Real Numbers

Adding Real Numbers

$$^-6 + 3 = {}^-3$$

Add.

1. $2\frac{3}{5} + (^-3\frac{2}{5}) + {}^-6 =$

2. $21 + 9 + (^-6) + 7 =$

3. $12 + (^-9) + 17 =$

4. $2.54 + {}^-5.87 + {}^-32.65 =$

5. $1 + {}^-5 + (^-5) + 1 =$

6. $21 + 3 + (^-13) + 22 =$

7. $3 + (^-3) + 4 + (^-5) =$

8. $3.3 + (^-3.4) + 5.5 =$

9. $3.6 + (^-2.5) + {}^-5.5 =$

10. $^-0.6 + (^-0.56) + 3 =$

11. $2 + 5 + {}^-3 =$

12. $4.524 + 7.342 =$

13. $^-7\frac{2}{4} + 2\frac{3}{4} =$

14. $34 + (^-13) + 18 + 0 + 34 =$

15. $8.43 + (^-10.98) + (^-3.23) =$

16. $2.54 + (^-5.21) + (^-6.34) =$

17. $^-2\frac{1}{3} + (^-5\frac{7}{10}) + (^-7) =$

18. $^-1\frac{2}{3} + (^-3\frac{3}{5}) + 4 =$

19. $2\frac{1}{2} + 6\frac{1}{2} =$

20. $4\frac{3}{5} + (^-3\frac{2}{5}) + (^-8) =$

CD-104316 • © Carson-Dellosa

Operations with Real Numbers

Subtracting Real Numbers

$$10 - (^-4) = 10 + 4 = 14$$

Subtract.

1. $9 - (^-32) =$

2. $^-99 - (^-42) =$

3. $\dfrac{3}{5} - \dfrac{7}{8} =$

4. $0 - 21 =$

5. $45 - 301 =$

6. $9.432 + 4.348 - 44.938 =$

7. $^-43 - 6 =$

8. $9 - (^-2) - 8 - 7 =$

9. $35 - 67 - 85 - 21 - 12 =$

10. $12 - 7 - (^-16) - 9 - (^-34) =$

11. $18 - (^-13) =$

12. $-\dfrac{2}{5} - \dfrac{3}{4} - (^-\dfrac{4}{5}) =$

13. $-\dfrac{4}{7} - \dfrac{1}{3} - (\dfrac{2}{3}) =$

14. $3.434 - 7.294 =$

15. $8 - 2.8 =$

16. $8 - (^-14) =$

17. $3.9 - 4.9 =$

18. $^-7 - (^-3) =$

19. $2.19 - 7.8 - 8.31 =$

20. $38 - 39 - (^-13) =$

Operations with Real Numbers

Subtracting Real Numbers

$$4 - (^-5) = 4 + 5 = 9$$

Subtract.

1. $^-9 - (^-5) =$

2. $321 - (^-34) =$

3. $\dfrac{2}{3} - \dfrac{4}{5} =$

4. $4 - (^-8) =$

5. $5.34 - 9.9 - 3.65 =$

6. $^-19 - 8 =$

7. $245 - 32 - (^-36) =$

8. $44 - 35 - 34 - 32 =$

9. $8 - (^-5) - 7 - 9 =$

10. $43 - 88 - 35 - 21 =$

11. $121 - 45 =$

12. $^-45 - 5 =$

13. $-\dfrac{2}{3} - \dfrac{1}{3} - (-\dfrac{1}{3}) =$

14. $-\dfrac{4}{5} - \dfrac{1}{2} - \dfrac{2}{5} =$

15. $4 - 12.9 =$

16. $7 - (^-33) =$

17. $3.4 - 7.4 =$

18. $2.456 - 4.345 - 5.457 =$

19. $23 - (^-21) =$

20. $4.346 - 0.4537 =$

CD-104316 • © Carson-Dellosa

Operations with Real Numbers

Multiplying Real Numbers

$$(^-2)(^-3) = 6$$

Multiply.

1. $4 \cdot 9 =$

2. $^-4 \cdot 12 =$

3. $(-\dfrac{5}{9})(8.8) =$

4. $(^-3)(0) =$

5. $(^-3)(^-9) =$

6. $6(23) =$

7. $(12)(^-3)(4) =$

8. $(^-5)(^-5)(^-5) =$

9. $(5)(2)(^-1) =$

10. $(7)(^-9)(^-12) =$

11. $(-\dfrac{2}{3})(^-1.6) =$

12. $^-7 \, (^-7) =$

13. $(54.2)(^-3.55) =$

14. $(2.22)(^-1.11) =$

15. $(7.44)(3.2)(4.3) =$

16. $(2.4)(^-1.4) =$

17. $(-\dfrac{3}{5})(\dfrac{3}{5}) =$

18. $(-\dfrac{4}{5})(2.2) =$

19. $^-8 \cdot 12 =$

20. $(0)(2)(^-213) =$

Operations with Real Numbers

Dividing Real Numbers

$$9 \div 4.5 = 2$$

Divide.

1. $\dfrac{49}{7} =$

2. $90 \div 15 =$

3. $(^-12) \div (9.9) =$

4. $(-\dfrac{2}{3}) \div (^-18) =$

5. $^-42 \div 7 =$

6. $45 \div (^-8) =$

7. $^-36 \div (4) =$

8. $(-\dfrac{3}{5}) \div (\dfrac{3}{5}) =$

9. $^-72 \div (9) =$

10. $^-21 \div (^-9) =$

11. $\dfrac{102}{17} =$

12. $0 \div (^-8) =$

13. $\dfrac{95}{5} =$

14. $\dfrac{63}{^-9} =$

15. $(^-3.4) \div (^-9.99) =$

16. $(^-56) \div (8.0) =$

17. $(-\dfrac{4}{6}) \div (36) =$

18. $32 \div (^-8) =$

19. $(-\dfrac{4}{5}) \div (^-1.6) =$

20. $520 \div (10) =$

 CD-104316 • © Carson-Dellosa

Name _____ Date _____

Operations with Real Numbers

Order of Operations

When solving an equation, be sure to follow the **order of operations**.

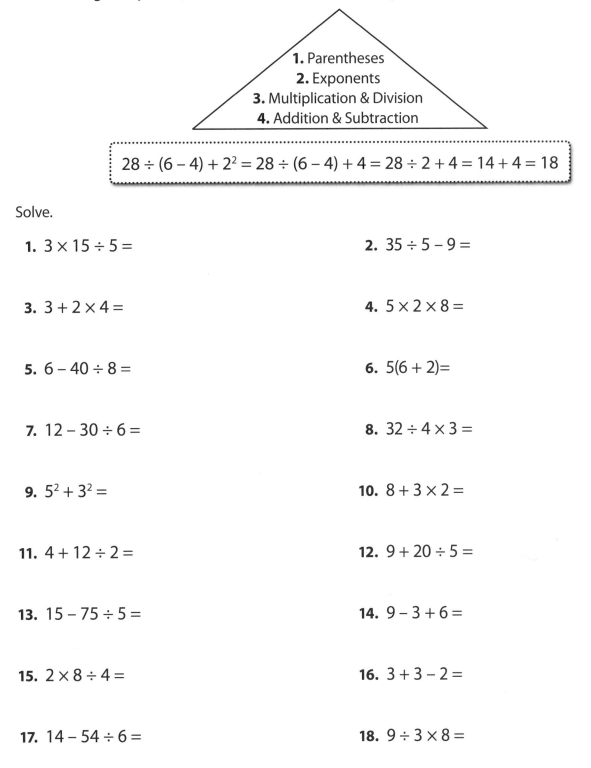

1. Parentheses
2. Exponents
3. Multiplication & Division
4. Addition & Subtraction

$28 \div (6 - 4) + 2^2 = 28 \div (6 - 4) + 4 = 28 \div 2 + 4 = 14 + 4 = 18$

Solve.

1. $3 \times 15 \div 5 =$

2. $35 \div 5 - 9 =$

3. $3 + 2 \times 4 =$

4. $5 \times 2 \times 8 =$

5. $6 - 40 \div 8 =$

6. $5(6 + 2) =$

7. $12 - 30 \div 6 =$

8. $32 \div 4 \times 3 =$

9. $5^2 + 3^2 =$

10. $8 + 3 \times 2 =$

11. $4 + 12 \div 2 =$

12. $9 + 20 \div 5 =$

13. $15 - 75 \div 5 =$

14. $9 - 3 + 6 =$

15. $2 \times 8 \div 4 =$

16. $3 + 3 - 2 =$

17. $14 - 54 \div 6 =$

18. $9 \div 3 \times 8 =$

Operations with Real Numbers

Order of Operations

When solving an equation, be sure to follow the **order of operations**.

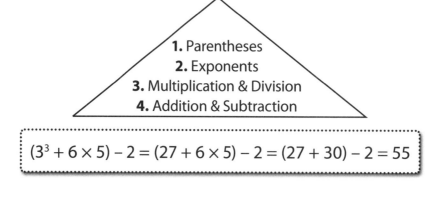

1. Parentheses
2. Exponents
3. Multiplication & Division
4. Addition & Subtraction

$(3^3 + 6 \times 5) - 2 = (27 + 6 \times 5) - 2 = (27 + 30) - 2 = 55$

Solve.

1. $(3^2 + 2 \times 3) \div 5 =$

2. $5^2 - 4^2 + 2 =$

3. $(4 + 2)^2 =$

4. $(11 - 8)^3 =$

5. $2(7 + 2) =$

6. $(9 - 7)^3 - (4 + 3) =$

7. $(14 - 6)2 =$

8. $4 + 3(12 - 9) =$

9. $5^2 - 2^3 =$

10. $3 \times 8 - (3 \times 2 + 7) =$

11. $(5^2 - 3 \times 5) \div 2 =$

12. $7 + 2^2(5 + 2) =$

13. $3 + 7^2 =$

14. $(2^2 + 3)^2 - 4 =$

15. $6 + 7 \times 3 - 9 \times 2 =$

16. $(2 \times 3) + (21 \div 7) =$

17. $7^2 - 2(3 \times 3 + 5) =$

18. $3 + (6 \times 2) =$

CD-104316 • © Carson-Dellosa

Operations with Real Numbers

Order of Operations

When solving an equation, be sure to follow the **order of operations**.

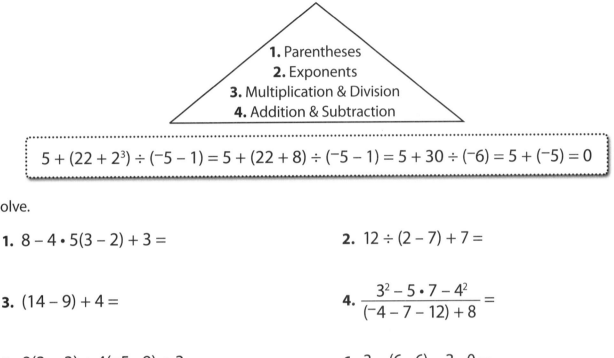

1. Parentheses
2. Exponents
3. Multiplication & Division
4. Addition & Subtraction

$5 + (22 + 2^3) \div (^-5 - 1) = 5 + (22 + 8) \div (^-5 - 1) = 5 + 30 \div (^-6) = 5 + (^-5) = 0$

Solve.

1. $8 - 4 \cdot 5(3 - 2) + 3 =$

2. $12 \div (2 - 7) + 7 =$

3. $(14 - 9) + 4 =$

4. $\dfrac{3^2 - 5 \cdot 7 - 4^2}{(^-4 - 7 - 12) + 8} =$

5. $9(3 \div 3) + 4(^-5 \cdot 9) \div 3 =$

6. $3 - (6 \cdot 6) - 3 \cdot 0 =$

7. $36 \div 9 - 8 + 21 \div 3 =$

8. $5(3 - 8) \cdot 3 + 8 - 3 =$

9. $3 \cdot 5 + 9 \cdot 7 =$

10. $\dfrac{(5 - 9)^2 + 2}{(7 - 8)^2 \cdot 3^2} =$

11. $4^2 + 3^2 - 7^2 =$

12. $\dfrac{3^2 - 10}{4^2 - 12} =$

13. $8^2 - \dfrac{26}{(4 + 9)} + 4 =$

14. $\dfrac{5 \cdot 7 - (3 + 4)}{^-2^2 - 2^2 + 3^2} =$

15. $\dfrac{4 + 2 \cdot 3 + 4 - 3}{2^2 \cdot 3^2 - 3} =$

16. $\dfrac{3 + 10 - 19 + 32}{3^2 - 1 + 2^2} =$

17. $12 \div [3 + (6 + 3)] =$

18. $3 \cdot (0 - 7) + 8 \div 2^2 =$

Operations with Real Numbers

Real-Number Operations with Absolute Value

$$-|5 - 11| = -|-6| = -6 \qquad |-4| + |-3| = 4 + 3 = 7$$

The **absolute value** of a number is its distance from zero.

For example: $|5| = 5 \qquad |-6| = 6 \qquad |0| = 0$

Simplify.

1. $|-3| =$

2. $|-14| =$

3. $9 + |-4| =$

4. $-5|4| + |5| =$

5. $|4| - |7| =$

6. $|21| + 9 =$

7. $23 + |8| =$

8. $|12| - |-15| =$

9. $7 - |-23| + |-7| =$

10. $|-6| + |8| =$

11. $-|-3 + 7| =$

12. $-|-5 + 10| =$

13. $|-9| + |23| =$

14. $|-17| - |-17| =$

15. $|1| - |0| + 6 =$

16. $|-67| - |-17| =$

17. $|4| - |-12| - 4 =$

18. $|3 - 13| =$

19. $|23| - |-12| =$

20. $|9| + |-9| =$

CD-104316 • © Carson-Dellosa

Name _____   Date _____

Variables and Equations

Substitution

Substitute and simplify. $a = 3, b = {}^-9, c = 5$

1. $b^2 + c^2 =$

2. ${}^-3b + (a + 2c)^2 =$

3. $2a^3 - (b + c)^2 =$

4. $(b + c)^2 =$

5. $(a + b)^2 =$

6. $abc =$

7. $(c - a)^2 =$

8. $4a - 6b - 2c =$

9. $(2c - a)^2 =$

10. $a^2 + b^3 =$

Substitute and simplify. $a = {}^-3, b = {}^-2, c = 5$

11. $5c + b^3 =$

12. $(a + b + c)^2 =$

13. $3(a + b)^2 =$

14. $c^2 - 2ab =$

15. $a^2 - (2b + c)^3 =$

16. $2c + 5a - 4b =$

17. $a^2 + b^2 =$

18. $2a - 4b =$

19. $a^2 - b^2 =$

20. $(a - b)^2 =$

Variables and Equations

Substitution

Substitute and simplify. $x = 2, y = 4, z = {}^-3$

1. $2z + 4xy =$

2. $(2x + y + 3z)^2 =$

3. $10xyz \div 5 =$

4. $5x + 2z =$

5. $(y + z)^3 =$

6. $2(6 + z) =$

7. $3(x + y)^2 =$

8. $2x + y + z =$

9. $(x - z) + y =$

10. $6y + 2xz =$

Substitute and simplify. $w = {}^-5, x = 4, y = 2, z = {}^-8$

11. $2wz - 3xy =$

12. $2y(z + x) =$

13. $wx + yz =$

14. $w^2 - x^2 =$

15. $5(w + x) + 3(7 + z) =$

16. $w + (x + 2y + z)^2 =$

17. $(z - w)^3 =$

18. $(w + x + y)^3 =$

19. $(2xy) - 2wz =$

20. $3w + 2z - xy + z^3 =$

CD-104316 • © Carson-Dellosa

Variables and Equations

Combining Like Terms

$$4x + 5y + (^-18x) = {}^-14x + 5y$$

Combine like terms.

1. $3yz + 5yz =$

2. $3a + 5 + a =$

3. $5x - 5y - 8y + 8x =$

4. $18x + 3x =$

5. $5 - (^-4k) =$

6. $7c - 12c =$

7. $13ab + (^-12ab) =$

8. $^-12x + (^-4x) =$

9. $^-10n - (^-13n) =$

10. $12b + (^-34b) =$

11. $4.7x - 5.9x =$

12. $4x^2 + (^-8y) + (^-3xy) + 5x^2 + 2xy =$

13. $4x + 3y + (^-5y) + 3xy + y =$

14. $2x - y + 2x + 3xy =$

15. $5x + 7x =$

16. $23x + 8 + 6x + 3y =$

17. $^-e + 8e =$

18. $2xy + 5x + 6xy + 3xy + (^-3x) =$

19. $7s + 5x - 8s =$

20. $4xy + 7xy + 6x^2y + 3xy^2 =$

Variables and Equations

Combining Like Terms

$5(x + 2) + (3x - 7y) + (2x + 4y) = 5x + 10 + 3x - 7y + 2x + 4y = 10x + 10 - 3y$

Combine like terms.

1. $^-n + 9n + 3 - 8 - 8n =$

2. $3(^-4x + 5y) - 3x(2 + 4y) =$

3. $5 - 4y + x + 9y =$

4. $^-2x + 3y - 5x - ^-8y + 9y =$

5. $6(a - b) - 5(2a + 4b) =$

6. $7(x + 5y) + 3(x + 5y) + 5(3x + 8y) =$

7. $12x + 6x + 9x - 3y + (^-7y) + y =$

8. $^-21x + (^-2x) =$

9. $4(x + 9y) - 2(2x + 4y) =$

10. $4(x + 5y) + (5x + y) =$

11. $6x + ^-2y^2 + 4xy^2 + 3x^2 + 5xy^2 =$

12. $^-2(c - d) + (c - 3d) - 5(c - d) =$

13. $3x + (^-3y) - (4x) + y =$

14. $^-3(4x + ^-2y) - 2(x + 3y) - 2(2x + 6y) =$

15. $2b + 3(2b + 8a) - 3(8b + 2a) =$

16. $3[2(^-y^2 + y) -3] - 3(2x + y) =$

17. $2 \cdot 4x \cdot 3y - 4x \cdot 7y =$

18. $5(3a^2 - 2b^2) + 3a(a + 3b^2) =$

19. $3c + 4d + 2c + 5d - 4c =$

20. $4(x^2 + 3y^2) - y(x^2 + 5y) =$

     CD-104316 • © Carson-Dellosa

Variables and Equations

Solving One-Step Equations (Addition and Subtraction)

$$12 + x = {}^-24$$
$$12 + ({}^-12) + x = {}^-24 + ({}^-12)$$
$$x = {}^-36$$

Solve each equation for the given variable.

1. ${}^-13 + b = 31$

2. $n + \frac{3}{8} = \frac{5}{8}$

3. $x - 17 = {}^-27$

4. $27 = v + ({}^-5)$

5. ${}^-4 = x - 3$

6. $c - 3 = 4.7$

7. $a + 5.7 = 18.9$

8. $12 - ({}^-u) = 17$

9. ${}^-200 = b + ({}^-73)$

10. ${}^-13 + x = 18$

11. ${}^-t + ({}^-7) = {}^-56$

12. $3 + x = 9$

13. $z + 3.5 = 4.7$

14. $12 + ({}^-g) = 10$

15. $y - 12 = 15$

16. $2\frac{1}{3} + r = 4\frac{2}{9}$

17. $x + 2 = 2(3 - 4)$

18. $s - 5 = 6 + ({}^-8)$

19. ${}^-13 = n + ({}^-39)$

20. $r = 4.4 + 3.9$

Variables and Equations

Solving One-Step Equations (Multiplication and Division)

$$3x = 15$$
$$\frac{3x}{3} = \frac{15}{3}$$
$$x = 5$$

$$-\frac{3}{4y} = {}^-6$$
$$-\frac{4}{3} \cdot -\frac{3}{4y} = {}^-6 \cdot -\frac{4}{3}$$
$$y = 8$$

Solve each equation for the given variable.

1. $12.8 = 4b$

2. $4b = {}^-36$

3. $^-13h = 169$

4. $-\frac{3}{4} = \frac{n}{16}$

5. $10x = {}^-100$

6. $4c = 288$

7. $7x = {}^-63$

8. $4y = {}^-48$

9. $6x = {}^-36$

10. $\frac{8}{k} = \frac{2}{5}$

11. $^-({}^-90) = {}^-45z$

12. $-\frac{x}{8} = \frac{1}{4}$

13. $^-50 = 2x$

14. $\frac{2}{n} = \frac{1}{9}$

15. $\frac{4}{x} = \frac{2}{9}$

16. $\frac{x}{6} = \frac{6}{9}$

17. $^-35c = 700$

18. $^-4x = {}^-20$

19. $-\frac{x}{6} = \frac{2}{3}$

20. $1.6c = 80$

CD-104316 • © Carson-Dellosa

Name _____ Date _____

Variables and Equations

Solving Basic Equations

$$4x + 4 = 12$$
$$4x + 4 - 4 = 12 - 4$$
$$4x = 8$$
$$x = 2$$

Solve each equation for the given variable.

1. $7x - 12 = 2$

2. $7a - 4 = 24$

3. $4b - 7 = 37$

4. $3c - 9 = 9$

5. $4.7 = {}^-3.4m - 5.5$

6. $8 - 9y = 35$

7. $8 - 12x = 32$

8. $1.3x + 5 = {}^-5.4$

9. $3(x + 4) + 5 = 35$

10. $0 = 25x + 75$

11. $3 - \frac{1}{5}x = {}^-7$

12. $5 - \frac{1}{2}x = {}^-9$

13. $2x = 6 + ({}^-18)$

14. $7 - \frac{1}{9}k = 32$

15. $32 = \frac{4}{6}x - 34$

16. $\frac{3}{12}x + 2 = 11$

17. $\frac{2x}{5} + 3 = 9$

18. $\frac{x}{3} - 8 = {}^-12$

19. $5(e + 5) = {}^-10$

20. $8 - \frac{1}{2}y = {}^-6$

Variables and Equations

Solving Basic Equations

$9x + 3 = 30$
$9x + 3 - 3 = 30 - 3$
$9x = 27$
$x = 3$

Solve each equation for the given variable.

1. $5t - 8 = {}^-28$

2. $4k + 7 = {}^-9$

3. $13x + 7 = {}^-32$

4. $2x + 12 = 6$

5. $7.2 + 4x = 19.2$

6. $2(w - 6) = 8$

7. $7h + 1 = {}^-13$

8. $3(c - 2) = 15$

9. $6x - 5 = {}^-41$

10. ${}^-3 + 2n = {}^-15$

11. $5e + ({}^-9) = 26$

12. $\dfrac{m}{3} - 7 = {}^-10$

13. $6x - 2 = 34$

14. ${}^-8(r - 2) = 40$

15. $5n - 8 = {}^-23$

16. $2 + (\frac{1}{5})x = {}^-7$

17. $5 - (\frac{1}{2})g = 12$

18. $3x - 4 = 14$

19. ${}^-6 = \dfrac{3u}{4} + 12$

20. $2(f + 7) - 8 = 22$

 CD-104316 • © Carson-Dellosa

Variables and Equations

Solving Basic Equations

$$12x + 3 = 123$$
$$12x + 3 - 3 = 123 - 3$$
$$12x = 120$$
$$x = 10$$

Solve each equation for the given variable.

1. $4(x - 6) = 8$

2. $4 + 3g = {}^-14$

3. $14a + 5 - 8a = {}^-1$

4. $4e + 6 - 11e = {}^-8$

5. ${}^-9r + 5 = {}^-22$

6. $2m - 9 - 8m = {}^-27$

7. $b + 9 - 2b = 6$

8. $4j - 9j + 3 = {}^-32$

9. $5(j - 4) + j = {}^-8$

10. $\dfrac{m}{4} + 6 = 2$

11. $3d - 5 - 2d = {}^-9$

12. ${}^-5 + 6d + 3 = 34$

13. $2k + 3(k + 4) = {}^-3$

14. $5(m - 3) + 2m = 27$

15. ${}^-j + 5j + 2 = {}^-14$

16. $7t - 3 + 4t = {}^-25$

17. $4(c + 2) = {}^-28$

18. $12k - 3(5 + 5) = 54$

19. $3e + 4e + 1 = 36$

20. ${}^-6r + 12 - 8r = {}^-2$

Variables and Equations

Solving Equations with Variables on Both Sides

$$6x - 7 = x + 33$$
$$6x - x - 7 = x - x + 33$$
$$5x - 7 + 7 = 33 + 7$$
$$5x = 40$$
$$x = 8$$

Solve each equation for the given variables.

1. $7 - 6a = 6 - 7a$

2. $3c - 12 = 14 + 5c$

3. $3x - 3 = {}^-3x + {}^-3$

4. $2x - 7 = 3x + 4$

5. $9a + 5 = 3a - 1$

6. $8(x - 3) + 8 = 5x - 22$

7. $5t + 7 = 4t - 9$

8. ${}^-10x + 6 = {}^-7x + {}^-9$

9. ${}^-7c + 9 = c + 1$

10. $2x + 6 = 5x - 9$

11. $\frac{5}{2}x + 3 = \frac{1}{2}x + 15$

12. $5 + 3x = 7(x + 3)$

13. $12m - 9 = 4m + 15$

14. $2(x - 4) + 8 = 3x - 8$

15. ${}^-6 - ({}^-2n) = 3n - 6 + 5$

16. $4(2y - 4) = 5y + 2$

17. $2(r - 4) = 5[r + ({}^-7)]$

18. $6(x - 9) = 4(x - 5)$

19. $4(t + 5) - 3 = 6t - 13$

20. $4e - 19 = {}^-3(e + 4)$

Variables and Equations

Problem Solving

> The sum of three times a number and 25 is 40. Find the number.
>
> $3x + 25 = 40$
>
> $3x + 25 - 25 = 40 - 25$
>
> $3x = 15$
>
> $x = 5$ The number is 5.

Write an equation for each word problem and solve it.

1. The difference of a number and $^-3$ is 8. Find the number.

   Equation _____   **Solution** _____

2. Twice a number added to 9 is 15. Find the number.

   Equation _____   **Solution** _____

3. Twelve subtracted from 3 times a number is 15. Find the number.

   Equation _____   **Solution** _____

4. The sum of 4 times a number and 5 is $^-7$. Find the number.

   Equation _____   **Solution** _____

5. The product of a number and 5 is 60. Find the number.

   Equation _____   **Solution** _____

6. The difference of 5 times a number and 6 is 14. Find the number.

   Equation _____   **Solution** _____

7. The sum of a number and $^-6$ is 10. Find the number.

   Equation _____   **Solution** _____

8. The quotient of a number and 4 is $^-12$. Find the number.

   Equation _____   **Solution** _____

Variables and Equations

Problem Solving

> The sum of four times a number and 14 is 74. Find the number.
>
> $4x + 14 = 74$
>
> $4x + 14 - 14 = 74 - 14$
>
> $4x = 60$
>
> $x = 15$ The number is 15.

Write an equation for each word problem and solve it.

1. Six times the difference of a number and 9 is 54. Find the number.

   Equation _____ **Solution** _____

2. The sum of 8 times a number and 3 is 59. Find the number.

   Equation _____ **Solution** _____

3. The sum of 5 times a number and ⁻11 is ⁻16. Find the number.

   Equation _____ **Solution** _____

4. Twelve times the sum of a number and ⁻8 is 48. Find the number.

   Equation _____ **Solution** _____

5. The sum of 5 times a number and 2 is ⁻13. Find the number.

   Equation _____ **Solution** _____

6. The sum of 7 times a number and 11 is 81. Find the number.

   Equation _____ **Solution** _____

7. Three times the sum of a number and ⁻2 is ⁻15. Find the number.

   Equation _____ **Solution** _____

8. Five times the sum of a number and 2 is 35. Find the number.

   Equation _____ **Solution** _____

 CD-104316 • © Carson-Dellosa

Variables and Equations

Solving Inequalities with Multiple Operations

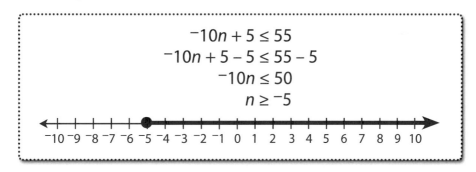

$$^-10n + 5 \le 55$$
$$^-10n + 5 - 5 \le 55 - 5$$
$$^-10n \le 50$$
$$n \ge {}^-5$$

Solve each inequality and graph its solution set.

1. $^-4(3t + 2) \le 4$

2. $10 - 5x - 20 \ge {}^-20$

3. $^-15 > 4x - 7 - 3x - 4$

4. $4x - 7 < 9$

5. $6x - 3 > 33$

6. $3(3c - 4) < 15$

7. $5x - 1 > 9$

8. $5 > 4x - 11$

Variables and Equations

Solving Inequalities with Variables on Both Sides

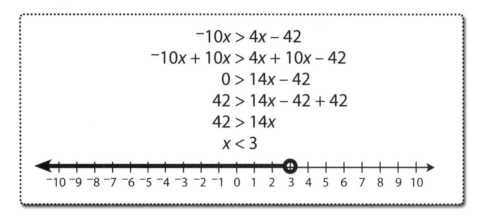

$$^{-}10x > 4x - 42$$
$$^{-}10x + 10x > 4x + 10x - 42$$
$$0 > 14x - 42$$
$$42 > 14x - 42 + 42$$
$$42 > 14x$$
$$x < 3$$

Solve each inequality and graph its solution set.

1. $7m + 9 \leq 6(m + 3)$

2. $3(2x + 4) \geq 7x + 8$

3. $2(k + 4) \leq 3(2k - 4)$

4. $5x + (^{-}3) > 2(3 + x)$

5. $5c + 2 < 2c + (^{-}7)$

6. $5x - 20 > 2x + 1$

7. $3(s - 4) \geq 4s - 12$

8. $^{-}9 - e > 3e + 11$

    CD-104316 • © Carson-Dellosa

Variables and Equations

Practice Solving Inequalities

Solve each inequality and graph its solution set.

1. $11 \leq 6y - 25$

2. $14 + 3x > 6x - 7$

3. $5x \geq {}^{-}20$

4. $^{-}13t > 52$

5. $6x - 4 > 2(x - 6)$

6. $12d < d + 11$

7. $14h \leq 112$

8. $4a - 3 \leq {}^{-}27$

9. $\dfrac{a}{4} + 3 \leq 5$

10. $r + 13 \geq 9$

Variables and Equations

Practice Solving Inequalities

Solve each inequality and graph its solution set.

1. $15e - 3 \leq 20e + 17$

```
←―+―+―+―+―+―+―+―+―+―+―+―+―+―+―+―+―+―+―+―+―→
  ⁻10 ⁻9 ⁻8 ⁻7 ⁻6 ⁻5 ⁻4 ⁻3 ⁻2 ⁻1  0  1  2  3  4  5  6  7  8  9  10
```

2. $13x \geq {}^{-}26$

```
←―+―+―+―+―+―+―+―+―+―+―+―+―+―+―+―+―+―+―+―+―→
  ⁻10 ⁻9 ⁻8 ⁻7 ⁻6 ⁻5 ⁻4 ⁻3 ⁻2 ⁻1  0  1  2  3  4  5  6  7  8  9  10
```

3. $7c - 8 \geq 6$

```
←―+―+―+―+―+―+―+―+―+―+―+―+―+―+―+―+―+―+―+―+―→
  ⁻10 ⁻9 ⁻8 ⁻7 ⁻6 ⁻5 ⁻4 ⁻3 ⁻2 ⁻1  0  1  2  3  4  5  6  7  8  9  10
```

4. $5n + 3 \geq {}^{-}12$

```
←―+―+―+―+―+―+―+―+―+―+―+―+―+―+―+―+―+―+―+―+―→
  ⁻10 ⁻9 ⁻8 ⁻7 ⁻6 ⁻5 ⁻4 ⁻3 ⁻2 ⁻1  0  1  2  3  4  5  6  7  8  9  10
```

5. $4 + 6r > {}^{-}8$

```
←―+―+―+―+―+―+―+―+―+―+―+―+―+―+―+―+―+―+―+―+―→
  ⁻10 ⁻9 ⁻8 ⁻7 ⁻6 ⁻5 ⁻4 ⁻3 ⁻2 ⁻1  0  1  2  3  4  5  6  7  8  9  10
```

6. $6d < 3d - 18$

```
←―+―+―+―+―+―+―+―+―+―+―+―+―+―+―+―+―+―+―+―+―→
  ⁻10 ⁻9 ⁻8 ⁻7 ⁻6 ⁻5 ⁻4 ⁻3 ⁻2 ⁻1  0  1  2  3  4  5  6  7  8  9  10
```

7. $^{-}2a < 10 + 3a$

```
←―+―+―+―+―+―+―+―+―+―+―+―+―+―+―+―+―+―+―+―+―→
  ⁻10 ⁻9 ⁻8 ⁻7 ⁻6 ⁻5 ⁻4 ⁻3 ⁻2 ⁻1  0  1  2  3  4  5  6  7  8  9  10
```

8. $4w > 2w + 8$

```
←―+―+―+―+―+―+―+―+―+―+―+―+―+―+―+―+―+―+―+―+―→
  ⁻10 ⁻9 ⁻8 ⁻7 ⁻6 ⁻5 ⁻4 ⁻3 ⁻2 ⁻1  0  1  2  3  4  5  6  7  8  9  10
```

9. $^{-}4.2 > 0.6x$

```
←―+―+―+―+―+―+―+―+―+―+―+―+―+―+―+―+―+―+―+―+―→
  ⁻10 ⁻9 ⁻8 ⁻7 ⁻6 ⁻5 ⁻4 ⁻3 ⁻2 ⁻1  0  1  2  3  4  5  6  7  8  9  10
```

10. $7k < {}^{-}35$

```
←―+―+―+―+―+―+―+―+―+―+―+―+―+―+―+―+―+―+―+―+―→
  ⁻10 ⁻9 ⁻8 ⁻7 ⁻6 ⁻5 ⁻4 ⁻3 ⁻2 ⁻1  0  1  2  3  4  5  6  7  8  9  10
```

CD-104316 • © Carson-Dellosa

Name _____ Date _____

Polynomials

Adding and Subtracting Polynomials

$$(x^2 + 4x + 2) - (2x^2 + 7x - 6) = {}^-x^2 - 3x + 8$$

Add or subtract the polynomials by combining like terms.

1. $(2x^2 + 3x + 2) - (6x^3 - 3x^2 + 8) - ({}^-2x^3 + 9x^2 + 7) =$

2. $(4y^2 - 9y) - ({}^-5y^2 + 8y - 8) =$

3. $({}^-3x^2 - 4x^3 - 1) - (2x^3 - 7x - 9) - (2x^3 - 2x^2 - 3) =$

4. $(6x^2 + 2x + 6) - (4x^2 - 2x + 3) + ({}^-5x^2 + 5x + 6) =$

5. $({}^-2x^3 + 3x^2 + 9) + ({}^-8x^3 - 2x^2 + {}^-4x) =$

6. $(2x^2 - 9x - 8) - (2x^3 - 7x^2 + {}^-2) =$

7. $(4x^3 - 2x^2 - 12) + (6x^2 + 3x + 8) =$

8. $(3x^4 - 3x + 1) - (4x^3 - 4x - 8) =$

9. $({}^-6x^2 - 3x^3 + 4) + ({}^-7x^3 + 2x + 4) - ({}^-3x^3 + 5x^2 + 2) =$

10. $(4x^2 + 6x + 3) + (3x^2 - 3x - 2) + ({}^-4x^2 + 3x - 9) =$

11. $(7x^2 - x - 5) - (3x^2 - 3x + 5) =$

12. $(x^3 - x^2 + 3) - (3x^3 - x^2 + 7) =$

13. $({}^-2x^2 + 4x - 12) + (5x^2 - 5x) =$

14. $(9x^2 - 7x + {}^-4) + (3x^3 - 4x + {}^-5) + ({}^-4x^2 - 2x - 5) =$

15. $(4x^3 - 5x^2 - 9) - (6x^3 - 5x - 4) - (5x^3 - 4x^2 - 10) =$

Polynomials

Raising Exponents to a Power and Multiplying Exponents

> Rule: $(x^a)^b = x^{ab}$ Example: $(x^2y^3)^3 = x^6y^9$
>
> Rule: $x^a \cdot x^b = x^{a+b}$ Example: $x^3 \cdot x^5 = x^8$

Multiply the polynomials.

1. $(^-4xy^3)^3 =$

2. $(x^2y^3)(x^3y) =$

3. $(^-6x^4y^6)^3 =$

4. $(5x^2y^4)^3 =$

5. $(6x^5y^4)^3 =$

6. $(2x)^4 =$

7. $(^-3x^2y)^3 =$

8. $(x^3y)^2 =$

9. $(^-2x^2y)^4 =$

10. $(x^2y^3)(x^3y^2) =$

11. $(^-4x^3y^3)^4 =$

12. $(3xy^3)(^-4x^2y^4)^2(xy^3) =$

13. $(^-3x^3y)^3 =$

14. $(^-2x^4y^5)^3 =$

15. $(3x^2y^3)^4 =$

16. $(6x^2y^3)^0 =$

17. $(x^3y^3)^3 =$

18. $(5xy^3)(^-5xy^2) =$

19. $(^-3x^2y^3)^2 =$

20. $(8xy)^2 =$

Polynomials

Multiplying Exponents

> Rule: $x^a \cdot x^b = x^{a+b}$ Example: $a^4 \cdot a^3 = a^7$

Multiply the polynomials.

1. $c \cdot c^2 \cdot c^3 =$

2. $e \cdot e^2 \cdot e^3 \cdot e^4 \cdot e^5 =$

3. $a^3 \cdot a^4 \cdot a^7 \cdot a =$

4. $(3xy^2)(2x^2y^3) =$

5. $(2a^2b)(4ab^2) =$

6. $(5f)(^-3f^3)(2f) =$

7. $(m^2n)(4mn^2)(mn) =$

8. $(4k^2)(^-3k)(3k^5) =$

9. $(^-2c^4)(4cd)(^-cd^2) =$

10. $(3x^3)(3x^4)(^-3x^2) =$

11. $(^-1)(x)(^-x^2)(x^3)(^-x^2) =$

12. $(3x^2)(^-3x^5) =$

13. $(c^2h)(3ch^3)(2c^3h^4) =$

14. $(^-4p^3)(^-4p^6)(^-2p^9) =$

15. $(12c^3)(2g^3)(4ch) =$

16. $(4x^2y^3)(x^3y)(^-x^2y^2) =$

17. $(^-4f^3)(^-3m^3) =$

18. $(2c^2d^2)(^-5cd^4) =$

19. $(4c^2)(^-5c^7) =$

20. $(3x)(^-4y^2)(6x^3y) =$

Polynomials

Dividing Exponents

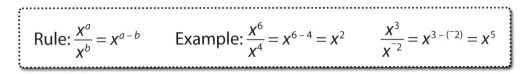

Rule: $\dfrac{x^a}{x^b} = x^{a-b}$ Example: $\dfrac{x^6}{x^4} = x^{6-4} = x^2$ $\dfrac{x^3}{x^{-2}} = x^{3-(^-2)} = x^5$

Divide the polynomials.

1. $\dfrac{-12m^5}{6m} =$

2. $\dfrac{x^3}{x^2} =$

3. $\dfrac{9a^3b^5}{-3ab^2} =$

4. $\dfrac{(6x^3)(3x^8)}{-12x^{10}} =$

5. $\dfrac{16c^3}{-4c^2} =$

6. $\dfrac{d^3}{d^2} =$

7. $\dfrac{-3p^8}{6p^2} =$

8. $\dfrac{-54c^2d^4}{-8cd} =$

9. $\dfrac{49r^{13}}{-7r^8} =$

10. $\dfrac{45k^7r^3}{-3k^5} =$

11. $\dfrac{-14c^{15}d^3}{-2c^9d} =$

12. $\dfrac{21k^9}{(3k)(7k^4)} =$

13. $\dfrac{(5k)(-8k^5)}{10k^3} =$

14. $\dfrac{(110c^3)(^-c^9)}{11c^5} =$

15. $\dfrac{24x^2y}{-4x^2} =$

16. $\dfrac{4x^2y^3z^4}{2xy^2z^3} =$

17. $\dfrac{9a^{11}}{a^3} =$

18. $\dfrac{(3xy)(4x^2y)}{-6xy^2} =$

19. $\dfrac{22y^5z^8}{2yz^7} =$

20. $\dfrac{b^{14}c^9}{b^5c^4} =$

CD-104316 • © Carson-Dellosa

Polynomials

Negative Exponents

Rule: $x^{-a} = \dfrac{1}{x^a}$ Example: $4^{-2} = \dfrac{1}{16}$ Example: $4x^{-2} = \dfrac{4}{x^2}$ Example: $(2x)^{-3} = \dfrac{1}{8x^3}$

$$4^{-2} = \dfrac{1}{4^2} = \dfrac{1}{16}$$ $$\dfrac{1}{(2x)^3} = \dfrac{1}{8x^3}$$

Simplify.

1. $4cd^{-5}$

2. $3a^{-6}$

3. $3a^4b^{-3}$

4. 4^{-5}

5. $(-2)^{-2}$

6. $(3xy)^{-1}$

7. $(3x)^{-3}$

8. $7x^{-3}$

9. $-2x^{-3}$

10. $(6y^2)^{-2}$

11. $\left(\dfrac{4}{5}\right)^{-2}$

12. $4m^3n^{-5}$

13. $(-11x^3y)^{-2}$

14. $(c^2d)^{-2}$

15. $14x^{-8}y$

16. $(-5x^3)^{-2}$

17. $\left(\dfrac{x^2}{y^3}\right)^{-2}$

18. $\left(\dfrac{2}{3}\right)^{-1}$

19. b^{-5}

20. c^{-7}

Polynomials

Products of Polynomials

$$4y(y - 3) = 4y^2 - 12y$$

Use the distributive property to multiply the polynomials.

1. $a(a + 8) =$

2. $5b(4b^3 - 6b^2 - 6) =$

3. $3x(x - 3) =$

4. $4a(2a + 6) =$

5. $y(y - 7) =$

6. $^-2x^2(5 - 3x + 3x^2 + 4x^3) =$

7. $4b(3 - b) =$

8. $2xy(2x - 3y) =$

9. $^-5y^2(7y - 8y^2) =$

10. $4x^2(3x^2 - x) =$

11. $x(x^2 + x + x) =$

12. $3b(4b^3 - 12b^2 - 7) =$

13. $(^-7x^3)(3x^2 - 1) =$

14. $^-5ab(6a - 4b) =$

15. $3x(x - 3) =$

16. $^-3x^2(4x^2 - 3x + 3) =$

17. $^-4x^2(3x^3 + 8x^2 + ^-9x) =$

18. $(3x^4 - 5x^2 - 4)(^-3x^3) =$

19. $5y(y^2 - 3y + 1) =$

20. $(3x^2 - 4x)(^-x) =$

CD-104316 • © Carson-Dellosa

Polynomials

Products of Polynomials

$(x - 3)(x^2 - 2x + 4) = x(x^2 - 2x + 4) - 3(x^2 - 2x + 4) = x^3 - 2x^2 + 4x - 3x^2 + 6x - 12$
$= x^3 - 5x^2 + 10x - 12$

Use the distributive property to multiply the polynomials.

1. $(3x + y)(3x - 2y) =$

2. $(x + 4)(x + 4) =$

3. $(3x + y)(2x^2 + 3x + 4y) =$

4. $5b(4b^3 - 4b^2 - 6) =$

5. $(x - 7)(x + 3) =$

6. $(x + y)(3x + y) =$

7. $(3x - 3)(x - 9) =$

8. $(2b - 8)(3b - 7) =$

9. $(3x^2 - x)(2x - x^2) =$

10. $(x + 3)(3 + x) =$

11. $(4a + 1)(4a + 1) =$

12. $(^-2x^3 + 4)(2x^2 + 5) =$

13. $(4x + 3)(x + 6) =$

14. $(4x^2 - 4y^2)(4x^2 + 4y^2) =$

15. $(x - y)(2x^2 + 2y^2) =$

16. $(5b - 2)(3b^3 + 5b^2 + 2) =$

17. $^-3x^2(4x^2 - 3x + 3) =$

18. $(3x^4 - 5x^2 - 4)(^-3x^3) =$

19. $x^2(3x^3 + 3x^2 + 3x) =$

20. $(3x + 3)(2x - 4) =$

Polynomials

Multiplying Binomials

> Rule: $(a + b)(a - b) = a^2 - b^2$
> Example: $(x - 3)(x + 3) = x^2 + 3x - 3x - 9 = x^2 - 9$

Use the FOIL method or DOTS rule to multiply the binomials.

1. $(2x + y)(2x - y) =$

2. $(b - 5)(b + 5) =$

3. $(x - y)(2x + 2y) =$

4. $(4b^2 - 4)(4b^2 + 4) =$

5. $(7x - 3y)(7x + 3y) =$

6. $(x + 6)(x - 6) =$

7. $(7x + y)(7x - y) =$

8. $(^-5x^2 + 3)(^-5x^2 - 3) =$

9. $(3a - b)(3a + b) =$

10. $(x + 2)(x - 2) =$

11. $(12b - 5)(12b + 5) =$

12. $(x - yz)(x + yz) =$

13. $(8x^2 - 12)(8x^2 + 12) =$

14. $(3x + 13)(3x - 2) =$

15. $(c + 2d)(c - 2d) =$

16. $(3b + 6)(3b - 6) =$

17. $(x^2 - 8x)(x^2 + 8x) =$

18. $(2x^2 - y^2)(2x^2 + y^2) =$

19. $(12 + b)(12 - b) =$

20. $(3x^2 - x)(3x^2 + x) =$

CD-104316 • © Carson-Dellosa

Polynomials

Squaring Binomials

Rules: $(a + b)^2 = a^2 + 2ab + b^2$
$(a - b)^2 = a^2 - 2ab + b^2$

Use the FOIL method or Squares of Binomial Formula to multiply the binomials.

1. $(x - 4y)^2 =$

2. $(3b - 3c)^2 =$

3. $(x - 2y)^2 =$

4. $(2x - 6y)^2 =$

5. $(7b^2 - 3c)^2 =$

6. $(4c + 9d)^2 =$

7. $(5x^2 - 5y)^2 =$

8. $(2x - 3y)^2 =$

9. $(^-4x + 3y)^2 =$

10. $(4m^2 - 2n)^2 =$

11. $(x^2 - 7y)^2 =$

12. $(4x^2 - 4y^2)^2 =$

13. $(7x - 5y)^2 =$

14. $(2b^2 - 2c^2)^2 =$

15. $(4a + b)^2 =$

16. $(2b + 5a)^2 =$

17. $(2x + 3v)^2 =$

18. $(5x + 7)^2 =$

19. $(3a - 7b)^2 =$

20. $(^-6x + 3y)^2 =$

Polynomials

Area and Perimeter

Find the perimeter of each polygon.

1.

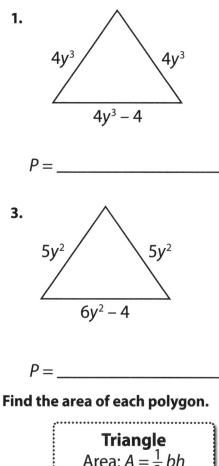

$4y^3$ $4y^3$

$4y^3 - 4$

$P =$ _____

2.

$x^2 + 3x - 1$

$x^2 - 3$ $x^2 - 3$

$x^2 + 3x - 1$

$P =$ _____

3.

$5y^2$ $5y^2$

$6y^2 - 4$

$P =$ _____

4.

$5x^2 + 2$

$4x^2$ $4x^2$

$5x^2 + 2$

$P =$ _____

Find the area of each polygon.

> **Triangle**
> Area: $A = \frac{1}{2} bh$
> **Rectangle**
> Area: $A = lw$
> **Square**
> Area: $A = s^2$

5.

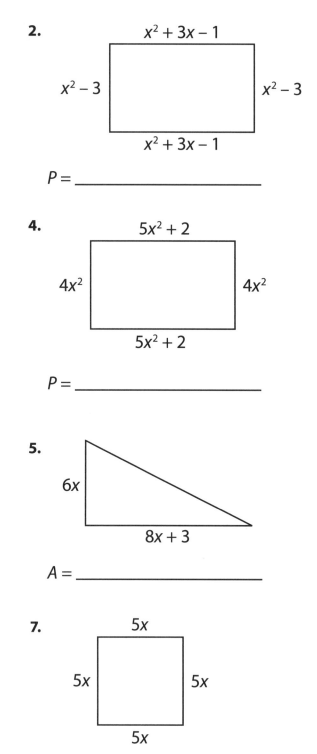

$6x$

$8x + 3$

$A =$ _____

6.

$x^2 + 3x - 1$

$3x$ $3x$

$x^2 + 3x - 1$

$A =$ _____

7.

$5x$

$5x$ $5x$

$5x$

$A =$ _____

                              CD-104316 • © Carson-Dellosa

Factoring

Factoring Monomials from Polynomials

To factor a polynomial, write the polynomial as a product of other polynomials.
   For example, $3x^2 - 6x$ can be written as $3x(x - 2)$.
   $3x$ is the Greatest Common Factor (GCF) of $3x^2$ and $6x$.
   $3x$ is a Common Monomial Factor of the terms of the binomial.
   $x - 2$ is a Binomial Factor of $3x^2 - 6$.

Factor.

1. $3x^2 - 12x^3 =$

2. $2x^3 - x^4 =$

3. $3a^5 - a^3 =$

4. $x^5 + 2x^2 =$

5. $24b^2 + 16b =$

6. $5x^3 - 7x^2 =$

7. $2x^3 + 6x^2 =$

8. $x^3 - 5x^2 =$

9. $15c - 3c^2 =$

10. $5x^5 - 12x^2 =$

11. $3x^5 + 4x^4 - 4x^2 =$

12. $9a^2 - 18a =$

13. $14b^3 - 7b^2 =$

14. $x^2 + x =$

15. $16a^5b^3 + 32a^4b =$

16. $x^3y^4 + x^2y^2 =$

17. $x^2 + x^4 + x^3 =$

18. $x^5 + 3x^2 =$

19. $x^2 + 3x^4 + 6x =$

20. $7x^2 - 21x^3 - 14x^4 =$

Factoring

Factoring Trinomials of the Form $x^2 + bx + c$

$$a^2 - 9a + 14 = (a - 7)(a - 2)$$

Factor.

1. $t^2 + 13t + 42 =$

2. $x^2 + x - 90 =$

3. $c^2 + c - 30 =$

4. $x^2 + 15xy + 44y^2 =$

5. $y^2 - 13y + 42 =$

6. $x^2 - x - 6 =$

7. $x^2 - 13x + 12 =$

8. $x^2 - 13x + 30 =$

9. $x^2 - 9x + 18 =$

10. $x^2 - 8x + 16 =$

11. $x^2 - 12xy + 32y^2 =$

12. $x^2 + 14x + 49 =$

13. $a^2 - 10ab - 24b^2 =$

14. $m^2 - 3mn + 2n^2 =$

15. $n^2 + 6n - 16 =$

16. $b^2 - 4b - 45 =$

17. $x^2 + 12x + 35 =$

18. $y^2 - 12y + 36 =$

19. $c^2 - 10c + 21 =$

20. $x^2 + 6x - 40 =$

                                                CD-104316 • © Carson-Dellosa

Factoring

Factoring Trinomials of the Form $x^2 + bx + c$

$$x^2 + 2x - 15 = (x + 5)(x - 3)$$

Factor.

1. $x^2 + 4x + 4 =$

2. $x^2 - 7x + 6 =$

3. $x^2 + 7x + 12 =$

4. $x^2 + 13x + 22 =$

5. $x^2 - 8x + 15 =$

6. $x^2 + 8xy - 33y^2 =$

7. $x^2 - 15x + 56 =$

8. $x^2 + 14x + 40 =$

9. $x^2 + 18x + 45 =$

10. $x^2 + 2x - 35 =$

11. $x^2 + 4x - 32 =$

12. $x^2 - 6x - 16 =$

13. $x^2 + 2xy - 63y^2 =$

14. $x^2 + 23x + 132 =$

15. $x^2 - 14x - 72 =$

16. $x^2 + 5xy + 6y^2 =$

17. $x^2 - xy - 2y^2 =$

18. $x^2 - 14xy + 24y^2 =$

19. $x^2 + 16x + 28 =$

20. $x^2 - 16x + 39 =$

Factoring

Factoring Trinomials of the Form $ax^2 + bx + c$

$2x^2 - 8x - 10 = 2(x^2 - 4x - 5) = 2(x - 5)(x + 1)$

Factor.

1. $12x^2 - 156x + 144 =$

2. $6x^2 - 15x + 6 =$

3. $2x^2 + 9x + 10 =$

4. $4x^2 - 18x + 20 =$

5. $3x^2 - 10x + 7 =$

6. $3x^2 - 5x - 12 =$

7. $3x^2 - 4x - 32 =$

8. $5x^2 + 25x + 30 =$

9. $3x^2 - 20x - 7 =$

10. $6x^2 - 15x - 21 =$

11. $7c^2 - 16c + 9 =$

12. $7x^2 - 26x - 8 =$

13. $2x^2 + 17x + 21 =$

14. $6a^2 - 21a + 15 =$

15. $2y^2 - 17y + 35 =$

16. $12x^2 - 6x - 18 =$

17. $4x^2 + 7x - 15 =$

18. $6x^2 - 25x - 25 =$

19. $4x^2 - 23x + 15 =$

20. $3x^2 + 19x + 20 =$

Factoring

Factoring Trinomials of the Form $ax^2 + bx + c$

$$2x^2 - 5x - 12 = (2x + 3)(x - 4)$$

Factor.

1. $6x^2 - 14x - 12 =$

2. $2x^2 + 13x + 6 =$

3. $4x^2 - 15x + 9 =$

4. $6x^2 - 21x - 12 =$

5. $6x^2 - 5x - 6 =$

6. $9x^2 - 9x - 28 =$

7. $5x^2 - 24x + 16 =$

8. $15x^2 + 11x - 14 =$

9. $4x^2 + 4x - 15 =$

10. $10x^2 - 28x - 6 =$

11. $14x^2 - 16x + 2 =$

12. $7x^2 + 17x + 6 =$

13. $12x^2 - 35x + 25 =$

14. $2x^2 - 2x - 40 =$

15. $4x^2 - 7x - 15 =$

16. $11x^2 - 122x + 11 =$

17. $2x^2 + 17x + 35 =$

18. $2x^2 + 7x + 3 =$

19. $4x^2 - x - 5 =$

20. $12x^2 + 9x - 3 =$

Factoring

Factoring Trinomials That Are Quadratic in Form

$$x^4 - x^2 - 12 = (x^2)^2 - (x^2) - 12 = (x^2 - 4)(x^2 + 3)$$

Factor.

1. $x^2y^2 + 10xy + 24 =$

2. $x^4y^4 - x^2y^2 - 12 =$

3. $2x^2 - 5x - 12 =$

4. $2x^4 + 16x^2 + 30 =$

5. $x^4 - 8x^2 + 15 =$

6. $7x^4 - 11x^2 - 6 =$

7. $2x^4 - 7x^2 - 15 =$

8. $y^4 + 6y^2 - 16 =$

9. $8x^4 - 23x^2 - 3 =$

10. $6a^6 - 5a^3b^3 - 25b^6 =$

11. $3x^4 + 20x^2 + 33 =$

12. $4x^4y^4 - 2x^2y^2 - 56 =$

13. $6x^2y^2 - 29xy + 23 =$

14. $x^4y^4 - 19x^2y^2 + 34 =$

15. $y^4 - y^2 - 12 =$

16. $x^2y^2 - 18xy + 32 =$

17. $2x^4y^4 - 17x^2y^2 - 30 =$

18. $2x^2 - 13x + 15 =$

19. $x^2y^2 - 8xy + 15 =$

20. $x^4y^4 - 8x^2y^2 + 12 =$

                                                    CD-104316 • © Carson-Dellosa

Factoring

Factoring Difference of Two Squares

Rule: $a^2 - b^2 = (a + b)(a - b)$ Example: $x^2 - 49 = (x + 7)(x - 7)$

Factor.

1. $a^2 - 4 =$

2. $b^2 - 9 =$

3. $1 - 9x^2 =$

4. $x^2 - 25 =$

5. $x^2y^2 - 36 =$

6. $x^2 - 100 =$

7. $y^2 - 81 =$

8. $c^2 - 16 =$

9. $a^2 - 49 =$

10. $49x^2 - 16y^4 =$

11. $16x^2 - 121 =$

12. $25 - x^2y^2 =$

13. $64 - x^4y^4 =$

14. $y^2 - 64 =$

15. $81x^2 - 4 =$

16. $16 - 81x^2 =$

17. $x^2y^2 - 121 =$

18. $49x^2 - 36 =$

19. $4x^2 - y^2 =$

20. $4x^2 - 1 =$

Factoring

Factoring Perfect Square Trinomials

> Rules: $a^2 + 2ab + b^2 = (a + b)^2$ $a^2 - 2ab + b^2 = (a - b)^2$
> Examples: $9x^2 + 6x + 1 = (3x + 1)^2$ $x^2 - 6x + 9 = (x - 3)^2$

Factor.

1. $x^2 - 18x + 81 =$

2. $x^2 - 4x + 4 =$

3. $x^2 - 16x + 64 =$

4. $b^2 - 10b + 25 =$

5. $x^2 + 14x + 49 =$

6. $x^2 - 2x + 1 =$

7. $c^2 - 6c + 9 =$

8. $x^2 - 4xy + 4y^2 =$

9. $a^2 + 12ab + 36b^2 =$

10. $49x^2 + 28x + 4 =$

11. $x^2 + 14x + 49 =$

12. $c^2 - 20c + 100 =$

13. $y^2 - 22y + 121 =$

14. $25a^2 - 40ab + 16b^2 =$

15. $9x^2 - 12x + 4 =$

16. $16x^2 - 40x + 25 =$

17. $9x^2 + 12x + 4 =$

18. $x^2 - 14x + 49 =$

19. $x^2 + 8x + 16 =$

20. $4x^2 + 4x + 1 =$

 CD-104316 • © Carson-Dellosa

Name _____ Date _____

Factoring

Factoring the Sum or Difference of Two Cubes

Rules: $x^3 + y^3 = (x + y)(x^2 - xy + y^2)$ $x^3 - y^3 = (x - y)(x^2 + xy + y^2)$
Examples: $x^3 + 8 = (x + 2)(x^2 - 2x + 4)$ $x^3 - 8 = (x - 2)(x^2 + 2x + 4)$

Factor.

1. $64x^3 + 1 =$ **2.** $8x^3 - 216 =$

3. $8x^3 + 27 =$ **4.** $x^3 + y^3 =$

5. $x^3 - 1000 =$ **6.** $1 - 64y^3 =$

7. $x^3 + 125 =$ **8.** $x^3 - 27 =$

9. $x^3y^3 + 64 =$ **10.** $64x^3 + 27y^3 =$

11. $27x^3 + y^3 =$ **12.** $x^3 - y^3 =$

13. $27x^3 - 64 =$ **14.** $27x^3 - 27 =$

15. $125a^3 - 8b^3 =$ **16.** $64x^3 - y^3 =$

17. $125x^3 - 64y^3 =$ **18.** $64x^3 + 27 =$

19. $27x^3 - 8y^3 =$ **20.** $x^3 - 8y^3 =$

Factoring

Solving Equations by Factoring

The **Multiplication Property of Zero**: The product of a number and zero is zero.
The **Principle of Zero Products**: If the product of two factors is zero, then at least one of the factors must be zero. This principle is used in solving equations.

$\quad$ Solve: $(x - 4)(x - 5) = 0$ $\quad$ If $(x - 4)(x - 5) = 0$, then $(x - 4) = 0$ or $(x - 5) = 0$.

$$x - 4 = 0 \quad x - 5 = 0 \qquad\qquad x = 4 \qquad\qquad x = 5$$

$$x = 4 \qquad x = 5$$

$$\frac{(4 - 4)(4 - 5) = 0}{(0)(^-1) = 0} \quad \frac{(5 - 4)(5 - 5) = 0}{(1)(0) = 0}$$

$\quad$ The solutions are 4 and 5. $\qquad\qquad\qquad (0)(^-1) = 0 \qquad\qquad (1)(0) = 0$

$$0 = 0 \qquad\qquad 0 = 0$$

Write the solutions for each variable.

1. $x(x + 6) = 0$

2. $b^2 - 81 = 0$

3. $(27 - y)(y - 2) = 0$

4. $z^2 - 1 = 0$

5. $(y - 4)(y - 8) = 0$

6. $y(y - 11) = 0$

7. $8t^2 - 32 = 0$

8. $x^2 - x - 6 = 0$

9. $x^2 - 4x - 21 = 0$

10. $m^2 - 144 = 0$

11. $(y + 5)(y + 6) = 0$

12. $(2x + 4)(x + 7) = 0$

13. $z^2 - 9 = 0$

14. $10x^2 - 10x = 0$

15. $2x^2 - 6x = x - 3$

16. $4y(3y - 2) = 0$

17. $(4y - 1)(y + 2) = 0$

18. $x^2 - 5x + 6 = 0$

CD-104316 • © Carson-Dellosa

Name _____ Date _____

Factoring

Problem Solving

The length of a rectangle is 5 inches longer than the width. The area of the rectangle is 50 square inches. Find the length and width of the rectangle.

Width of rectangle: w

Length of rectangle: $w + 5$

$A = lw$

$50 = (w + 5)(w)$ Since the width cannot be a negative number,

$50 = w^2 + 5w$ the width is 5.

$0 = w^2 + 5w - 50$

$0 = (w + 10)(w - 5)$ $l = 5 + 5 = 10$

$w + 10 = 0$ or $w - 5 = 0$

$w = {}^-10$ $w = 5$ The length is 10, and the width is 5.

For each word problem, write an equation and solve it.

1. The sum of twice a number and its square is 143. Find the numbers.

Equation _____ Solution _____

2. The sum of a number and its square is 42. Find the numbers.

Equation _____ Solution _____

3. The sum of a number and its square is 56. Find the numbers.

Equation _____ Solution _____

4. The sum of a number and its square is 90. Find the numbers.

Equation _____ Solution _____

5. The square of a number is 80 more than 2 times the number. Find the numbers.

Equation _____ Solution _____

6. The square of a number is 48 more than 2 times the number. Find the numbers.

Equation _____ Solution _____

7. For what numbers is the sum of a number and its square equal to 110?

Equation _____ Solution _____

Name _____ Date _____

Factoring

Problem Solving

The length of a rectangle is 3 inches longer than the width. The area of the rectangle is 40 square inches. Find the length and width of the rectangle.

Width of rectangle: w

Length of rectangle: $w + 3$

$A = lw$

$40 = (w + 3)(w)$ Since the width cannot be a negative number,

$40 = w^2 + 3w$ the width is 5.

$0 = w^2 + 3w - 40$

$0 = (w + 8)(w - 5)$ $l = 5 + 3 = 8$

$w + 8 = 0$ or $w - 5 = 0$

$w = {}^-8 \quad w = 5$ The length is 8, and the width is 5.

For each word problem, write an equation and solve it.

1. The area of a square is 121m². Find the length of the sides of the square.

   Equation _____ Solution _____

2. The area of a rectangle is 72 m². Its length is twice its width. Find the length and width of the rectangle.

   Equation _____ Solution _____

3. The area of a rectangle is 36 cm². Its width is 4 times its length. Find the length and width of the rectangle.

   Equation _____ Solution _____

4. The width of a rectangle is 5 more than twice its length. The area of the rectangle is 33 in.². Find the dimensions of the rectangle.

   Equation _____ Solution _____

5. The length of a rectangle is 4 more than twice its width. The area of the rectangle is 96 ft.². Find its dimensions.

   Equation _____ Solution _____

Name _____ Date _____

Rational Expressions

Dividing Monomials

$$\frac{35x^9y^6}{5x^7y^8} = \frac{35}{5} \cdot x^{9-7} \, y^{6-8} = \frac{7x^2}{y^2}$$

Simplify.

1. $\dfrac{a^3}{a^5}$

2. $\dfrac{a^5b^2}{2a^2}$

3. $\dfrac{13m^6n^7}{39m^3n^5}$

4. $\dfrac{9x^8y^7z^8}{18x^5y^5z^4}$

5. $\dfrac{7c^2d^3}{28cd^2}$

6. $\dfrac{10a^6b^8}{40a^2b^2}$

7. $\dfrac{18a^6b^2c^6}{36a^4bc^2}$

8. $\dfrac{5x^3y^2z^2}{5x^2yz}$

9. $\dfrac{45x^9y^{10}z^5}{51x^9y^8z^3}$

10. $\dfrac{16x^2y^4}{4x^2y^3}$

11. $\dfrac{18x^6y^3z^4}{12x^3y^2z^3}$

12. $\dfrac{72x^5y^5z^6}{8x^4yz^3}$

13. $\dfrac{18a^9b^3}{54a^2b^2}$

14. $\dfrac{44x^8y^2}{11x^7yz}$

Name _____ Date _____

Rational Expressions

Simplifying Rational Expressions

$$\frac{a^2 + 6a + 9}{a} = \frac{a^2}{a} + \frac{6a}{a} + \frac{9}{a}$$
$$= a + 6 + \frac{9}{a}$$

Simplify.

1. $\dfrac{24y^5 + 12y^3}{6y}$

2. $\dfrac{3xc^2 + 6c^2d}{3cd}$

3. $\dfrac{3x^4y^5 + 12x^2y^3 - 18x^2}{x^2y}$

4. $\dfrac{18x + 36}{9}$

5. $\dfrac{10a^6b^8 + 8a^3b^5}{ab}$

6. $\dfrac{12a^2 - 2a + 12}{2a}$

7. $\dfrac{2x^3y^2 - 2x^3y^4 - 4x^5y^3}{2x^3y^3}$

8. $\dfrac{9x^4 - 3x^5 - 12x^4y^3}{3xy^3}$

9. $\dfrac{6x^8 + 6x + 3}{3x^2}$

10. $\dfrac{x^3y^3 + x - y}{x^3y}$

11. $\dfrac{m^6n^7 + m - n}{m^2n}$

12. $\dfrac{5x^3 + 3x}{x}$

13. $\dfrac{12a^3 - 9a^3 - 3a}{-30}$

14. $\dfrac{18x^3 - 9x^2 - 3x}{-3}$

 CD-104316 • © Carson-Dellosa

Rational Expressions

Dividing Polynomials

Simplify: $(x^2 + 6x + 5) \div (x + 1)$

$$\frac{(x^2 + 6x + 5)}{(x + 1)}$$

$$
\begin{array}{r}
x + 5 \\
x + 1 \overline{)\, x^2 + 6x + 5} \\
-x^2 + 1x \\
\hline
5x + 5 \\
-5x + 5 \\
\hline
0
\end{array}
$$

Divide by using long division.

1. $(x^2 + 5x + 6) \div (x + 3) =$

2. $(x^2 + 4x - 21) \div (x - 3) =$

3. $(x^2 - 3x - 40) \div (x + 5) =$

4. $(x^2 - x - 42) \div (x + 6) =$

5. $(x^2 - 8x + 16) \div (x - 4) =$

6. $(x^2 + 2x - 35) \div (x + 7) =$

7. $(x^2 - 6x + 9) \div (x - 3) =$

8. $(x^2 + 5x + 4) \div (x + 1) =$

9. $(x^2 + 7x + 10) \div (x + 2) =$

10. $(x^2 + 9x + 8) \div (x + 8) =$

Rational Expressions

Dividing Polynomials

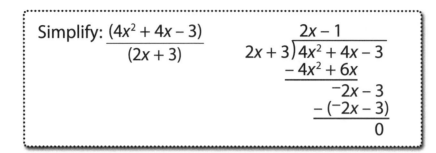

Simplify: $\dfrac{(4x^2 + 4x - 3)}{(2x + 3)}$

$$
\begin{array}{r}
2x - 1 \\
2x + 3 \overline{)\,4x^2 + 4x - 3} \\
-\ 4x^2 + 6x \\
\hline
^-2x - 3 \\
-\ (^-2x - 3) \\
\hline
0
\end{array}
$$

Divide by using long division.

1. $\dfrac{x^2 - 9x + 8}{x - 1} =$

2. $\dfrac{2x^2 - 5x - 3}{x - 3} =$

3. $\dfrac{4x^2 - 7x - 2}{4x + 1} =$

4. $\dfrac{2x^2 - 7x - 15}{x - 5} =$

5. $\dfrac{21x^2 + 22x - 8}{3x + 4} =$

6. $\dfrac{3x^2 - 27}{x + 3} =$

7. $\dfrac{9x^2 - 27x - 36}{x - 4} =$

8. $\dfrac{5x^2 + 43x - 18}{x + 9} =$

9. $\dfrac{x^2 - 4x - 45}{x + 5} =$

10. $\dfrac{2x^2 - x - 21}{x + 3} =$

Rational Expressions

Dividing Polynomials by Synthetic Division

Simplify: $(2x^3 + 3x^2 - 4x + 8) \div (x + 3)$

$$
\begin{array}{r|rrrr}
-3 & 2 & 3 & -4 & 8 \\
   &   & -6 & 9 & -15 \\
\hline
   & 2 & -3 & 5 & -7
\end{array}
$$

$$= 2x^2 - 3x + 5 - \dfrac{7}{x + 3}$$

Divide by using synthetic division.

1. $(x^2 + x - 2) \div (x + 2) =$

2. $(5x^2 - 12x - 9) \div (x - 3) =$

3. $(3x^2 - 5) \div (x - 1) =$

4. $(3x^3 + 8x^2 + 9x + 10) \div (x + 2) =$

5. $(x^3 - 4x^2 - 36x - 16) \div (x + 4) =$

6. $(3x^2 - 7x + 6) \div (x - 3) =$

7. $(4x^2 + 9x + 6) \div (x + 1) =$

8. $(3x^3 - 13x^2 - 13x + 15) \div (x - 5) =$

9. $(2x^3 - 12x^2 + 5x - 27) \div (x - 6) =$

10. $(4x^2 + 23x + 28) \div (x + 4) =$

11. $(3x^2 - 75) \div (x - 5) =$

12. $(3x^2 + 19x + 20) \div (x + 5) =$

13. $(2x^2 + 7x - 10) \div (x + 1) =$

14. $(x^2 + 14x + 45) \div (x + 5) =$

Rational Expressions

Multiplying Rational Expressions

$$\frac{4(x^2 - 16)}{12x^2 + 48x} = \frac{4(x + 4)(x - 4)}{12x(x + 4)} = \frac{x - 4}{3x}$$

Simplify.

1. $\dfrac{x^2 + x - 6}{x + 1} \cdot \dfrac{x + 1}{x^2 - 9} =$

2. $\dfrac{x^2 - 1}{x^2 - 2x - 3} \cdot \dfrac{x + 4}{6x - 6} =$

3. $\dfrac{4x - 4}{x^2 - 9} \cdot \dfrac{x + 3}{x - 1} =$

4. $\dfrac{12x^2y^4}{36ab^3} \cdot \dfrac{6a^2v^3}{48xy^4} =$

5. $\dfrac{x + 2}{x - 3} \cdot \dfrac{x^2 - 8x + 15}{5x - 25} =$

6. $\dfrac{x^2 - 2x - 8}{x^2 - 4} \cdot \dfrac{x - 2}{x + 3} =$

7. $\dfrac{x^2 + 6x + 8}{x^2 - 16} \cdot \dfrac{3x - 12}{4x + 4} =$

8. $\dfrac{x^2 + 3x + 2}{x + 7} \cdot \dfrac{x^2 + 9x + 14}{x^2 + 4x + 4} =$

9. $\dfrac{2x^2 - 32}{2x + 8} \cdot \dfrac{x^2 - 9}{x^2 - 3x - 4} =$

10. $\dfrac{14x^2y^4}{42a^2b^4} \cdot \dfrac{28a^2b^3}{35x^3y^4} =$

11. $\dfrac{x^2 - 100}{x - 5} \cdot \dfrac{x + 5}{x^2 - 5x - 50} =$

12. $\dfrac{x^2 - 12x + 35}{x^2 - 5x - 14} \cdot \dfrac{x^2 + 7x + 10}{x^2 - 25} =$

13. $\dfrac{9x^2 - 25}{4x^2 + 4x - 3} \cdot \dfrac{40x^2 - 10x}{3x + 5} =$

14. $\dfrac{x + 4}{6x^2 - 24} \cdot \dfrac{2x^3 - 8x}{x^2 + 4x} =$

 CD-104316 • © Carson-Dellosa

Rational Expressions

Dividing Rational Expressions

Simplify.

1. $\dfrac{x-7}{x+2} \div \dfrac{x^2-49}{x^2+9x+14} =$

2. $\dfrac{x+2}{4x(x-6)} \div \dfrac{x^2-4}{8x(x-6)} =$

3. $\dfrac{x^2-4}{4x+4} \div \dfrac{x-2}{x+1} =$

4. $\dfrac{x+2}{x+3} \div \dfrac{x^2-4}{x-2} =$

5. $\dfrac{2x^2+12x+18}{x^2+5x-6} \div \dfrac{2x+6}{x-1} =$

6. $\dfrac{2x^2+6x}{x^2+2x} \div \dfrac{x^2-9}{4x-12} =$

7. $\dfrac{15x^4y^2}{5xy} \div \dfrac{10x^3y}{5y^2} =$

8. $\dfrac{x^2+8x}{x^2+14x+48} \div \dfrac{x^2+x}{x^2} =$

9. $\dfrac{3x^2+6x}{x^2+6x} \div \dfrac{x^2-4}{2x-4} =$

10. $\dfrac{x^2-16}{x^2+7x+12} \div \dfrac{5x-20}{x+3} =$

11. $\dfrac{x^2-7x}{x^2-14x+49} \div \dfrac{2x^2+6x}{x^2+x-56} =$

12. $\dfrac{x^2+9x-10}{x^2+5x-14} \div \dfrac{3x+30}{2x-4} =$

13. $\dfrac{27x^6y^2}{9x^3y} \div \dfrac{4x^5y^3}{16x^4y^2} =$

14. $\dfrac{24a^4b^2}{8a^2b} \div \dfrac{12ab^3}{16a^3b} =$

Rational Expressions

Adding and Subtracting Rational Expressions

$$\frac{7x-12}{2x^2+5x-12} - \frac{3x-6}{2x^2+5x-12} = \frac{(7x-12)-(3x-6)}{2x^2+5x-12} = \frac{7x-12-3x+6}{2x^2+5x-12} =$$

$$\frac{2(2x-3)}{(2x-3)(x+4)} = \frac{2(2x-3)}{(2x-3)(x+4)} = \frac{2}{x+4}$$

Simplify.

1. $\dfrac{2}{x+2} + \dfrac{6x}{x^2-4} =$

2. $\dfrac{7a}{a-4} + \dfrac{5}{a+4} =$

3. $\dfrac{3}{4xy} + \dfrac{14}{3xy} - \dfrac{9}{2xy} =$

4. $\dfrac{x}{2x-5} + \dfrac{3}{2x-5} =$

5. $\dfrac{x}{x-4} + \dfrac{4}{x^2-x-12} =$

6. $\dfrac{4}{3x-8} - \dfrac{x}{4x-7} =$

7. $-\dfrac{4}{2x^2} + \dfrac{5}{2x^2} + \dfrac{8}{3x^2} =$

8. $-\dfrac{4x}{x^2+x-2} + \dfrac{4x}{x^2+x-2} =$

9. $\dfrac{11x}{x^2-6x-7} + \dfrac{5x}{x^2+9x+8} =$

10. $\dfrac{3x}{x^2-4} + \dfrac{5x}{x^2-4} =$

11. $-\dfrac{10}{4x^2} + \dfrac{6}{4x^2} + \dfrac{8}{4x^2} =$

12. $\dfrac{5}{2xy} + \dfrac{5}{4xy} - \dfrac{12}{6xy} =$

Rational Expressions

Solving Fractional Equations

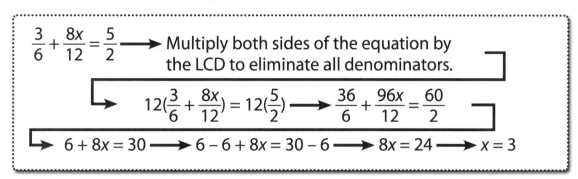

Solve.

1. $\dfrac{2}{17} = \dfrac{x-6}{x+9}$

2. $\dfrac{3}{4} = \dfrac{x+2}{x-8}$

3. $1 - \dfrac{4}{y} = 5$

4. $\dfrac{6}{x} - \dfrac{2}{8} = \dfrac{x}{8}$

5. $\dfrac{x}{2} + \dfrac{5}{6} = \dfrac{x}{3}$

6. $\dfrac{(x-4)}{30} = \dfrac{1}{5}$

7. $17 - \dfrac{3}{x} = 8$

8. $\dfrac{x+2}{x+7} = \dfrac{7}{12}$

9. $\dfrac{6}{(x+4)} = \dfrac{x-3}{22-x}$

10. $\dfrac{x+1}{x+5} = \dfrac{5}{9}$

11. $\dfrac{x+7}{x-9} = \dfrac{28}{12}$

12. $\dfrac{x-5}{x-1} = \dfrac{1}{5}$

13. $\dfrac{x-2}{x+6} = \dfrac{1}{9}$

14. $3 - \dfrac{9}{y} = 30$

Ratios and Proportions

Proportions

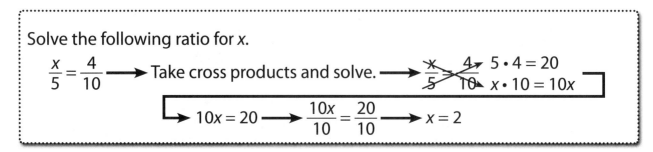

Solve the following ratio for x.

$\frac{x}{5} = \frac{4}{10}$ ⟶ Take cross products and solve. ⟶ $\frac{x}{5} \times \frac{4}{10}$ $\begin{array}{l} 5 \cdot 4 = 20 \\ x \cdot 10 = 10x \end{array}$

⟶ $10x = 20$ ⟶ $\frac{10x}{10} = \frac{20}{10}$ ⟶ $x = 2$

Solve.

1. $\frac{4}{(x-3)} = \frac{28}{49}$

2. $\frac{(5+x)}{10} = \frac{2}{5}$

3. $\frac{x}{30} = \frac{7}{10}$

4. $\frac{(x-2)}{16} = \frac{x}{4}$

5. $\frac{2}{x} = \frac{6}{30}$

6. $\frac{(x+1)}{7} = \frac{6}{14}$

7. $\frac{x}{15} = \frac{5}{75}$

8. $\frac{x}{20} = \frac{2}{10}$

9. $\frac{x}{6} = \frac{(x-3)}{12}$

10. $\frac{x}{5} = \frac{12}{6}$

11. $\frac{6}{(x+5)} = \frac{18}{24}$

12. $\frac{5}{15} = \frac{x}{9}$

13. $\frac{x+x}{10} = \frac{5}{2}$

14. $\frac{x}{3} = \frac{12}{27}$

CD-104316 • © Carson-Dellosa

Ratios and Proportions

Problem Solving with Proportions

Three liters of soda cost $3.00. At this rate, how much would 10 liters of soda cost?
To find the cost, write and solve a ratio using x to represent the cost.

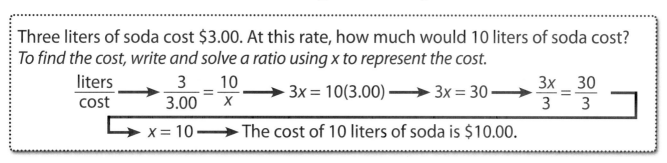

$$\frac{\text{liters}}{\text{cost}} \longrightarrow \frac{3}{3.00} = \frac{10}{x} \longrightarrow 3x = 10(3.00) \longrightarrow 3x = 30 \longrightarrow \frac{3x}{3} = \frac{30}{3}$$

$$\longrightarrow x = 10 \longrightarrow \text{The cost of 10 liters of soda is }\$10.00.$$

Solve.

1. The real estate tax for a house that costs $56,000 is $1,400. At this rate, what is the value of a house for which the real estate tax is $1,800?

2. A copy machine can print 120 pages per minute. At this rate, how many minutes are required to make 840 copies?

3. One hundred thirty-six tiles are required to tile a 36 ft.² area. At this rate, how many tiles are required to tile a 288 ft.² area?

4. Two gallons of fruit juice will serve 35 people. How much fruit juice is necessary to serve 105 people?

5. A stock investment of $4,000 earns $360 each year. At the same rate, how much money can a person earn if he invests $6,000?

Name _____ Date _____

Ratios and Proportions

Problem Solving with Proportions

Three gallons of gasoline costs $3.00. At this rate, how much would 6 gallons of gasoline cost? *To find the cost, write and solve a proportion using x to represent the cost.*

$$\frac{\text{gallons}}{\text{cost}} \longrightarrow \frac{3}{\$3} = \frac{6}{x} \longrightarrow 3x = 18 \longrightarrow \frac{3x}{3} = \frac{18}{3} \longrightarrow x = 6$$

The cost of 6 gallons of gasoline is $6.00.

Solve.

1. An investment of $36,000 earns $900 each year. At the same rate, how much money must be invested to earn $1,200 each year?

2. The sales tax on a $15,000 car is $540. At this rate, what is the tax on a $32,000 car?

3. Six gallons of paint will cover 120 doors. At this rate, how many gallons of paint are needed to cover 480 doors?

4. A lawnmower can cut 1 acre on 0.5 gallons of gasoline. At this rate, how much gasoline is needed to cut 3.5 acres?

5. An aerobics instructor burns 400 calories in 1 hour. How many hours would the instructor have to do aerobics to burn 660 calories?

                                                        CD-104316 • © Carson-Dellosa

Name _____   Date _____

Graphing

Graphing Ordered Pairs

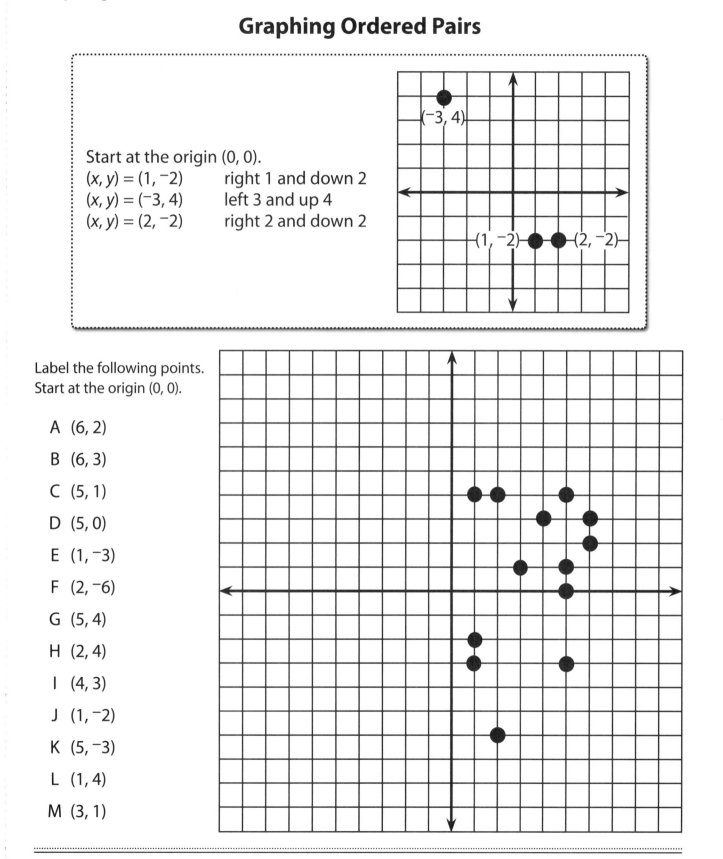

Start at the origin (0, 0).
$(x, y) = (1, ^-2)$ right 1 and down 2
$(x, y) = (^-3, 4)$ left 3 and up 4
$(x, y) = (2, ^-2)$ right 2 and down 2

Label the following points.
Start at the origin (0, 0).

A (6, 2)

B (6, 3)

C (5, 1)

D (5, 0)

E (1, ⁻3)

F (2, ⁻6)

G (5, 4)

H (2, 4)

I (4, 3)

J (1, ⁻2)

K (5, ⁻3)

L (1, 4)

M (3, 1)

Graphing

Graphing Ordered Pairs

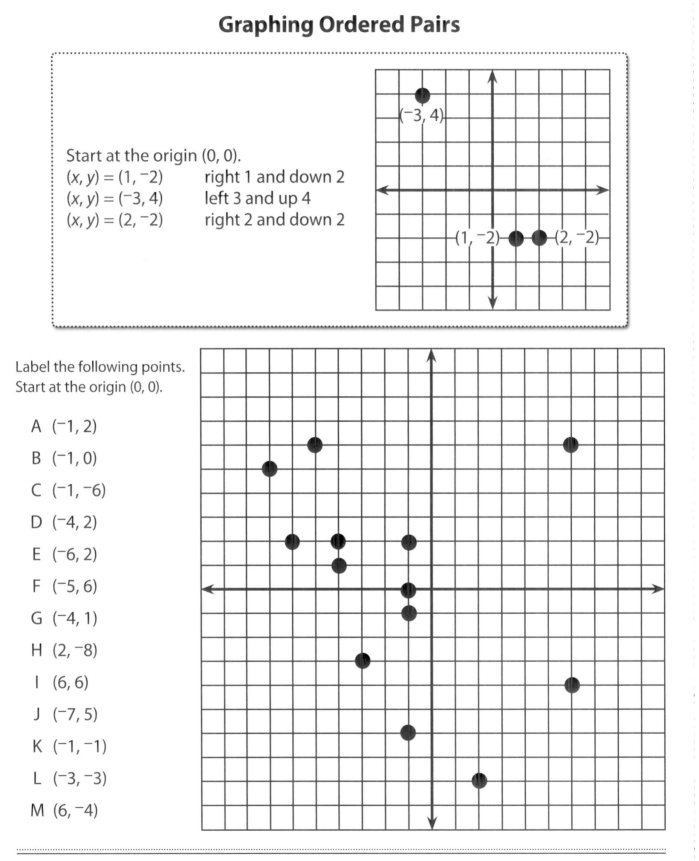

Start at the origin (0, 0).
$(x, y) = (1, {}^-2)$ right 1 and down 2
$(x, y) = ({}^-3, 4)$ left 3 and up 4
$(x, y) = (2, {}^-2)$ right 2 and down 2

Label the following points.
Start at the origin (0, 0).

A $({}^-1, 2)$

B $({}^-1, 0)$

C $({}^-1, {}^-6)$

D $({}^-4, 2)$

E $({}^-6, 2)$

F $({}^-5, 6)$

G $({}^-4, 1)$

H $(2, {}^-8)$

I $(6, 6)$

J $({}^-7, 5)$

K $({}^-1, {}^-1)$

L $({}^-3, {}^-3)$

M $(6, {}^-4)$

CD-104316 • © Carson-Dellosa

Graphing

Plotting Points

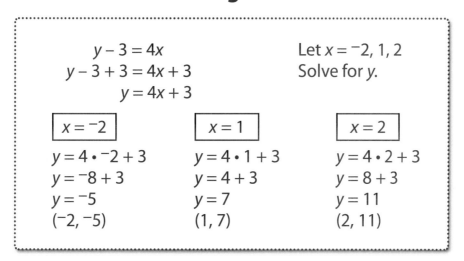

Solve each equation for *y*. Use the given values for *x* to find the values for *y*. Write answers as ordered pairs.

1. $6x - y = {}^-18$ Let $x = 2, 3, {}^-2$

2. ${}^-x = y - 8$ Let $x = {}^-1, {}^-2, 1$

3. $2x + y = {}^-4$ Let $x = {}^-3, 2, 4$

4. $6x + y = 3$ Let $x = {}^-4, 0, 2$

5. $4 - y = 3x$ Let $x = {}^-3, 1, {}^-2$

6. $2 = y - 6x$ Let $x = {}^-1, 0, 2$

7. $2x + y = {}^-12$ Let $x = {}^-2, 0, 3$

Graphing

Graphing Ordered Pairs

Solve for y in each equation. Choose 3 values for x and find the values for y. Graph the 3 ordered pairs and draw a line connecting them.

$$y - 3 = 2x$$
$$y - 3 + 3 = 2x + 3$$
$$y = 2x + 3$$

x	y
$^-2$	$^-1$
0	3
1	5

$y = 2 \cdot {}^-2 + 3$ $\qquad$ $y = 2 \cdot 0 + 3$ $\qquad$ $y = 2 \cdot 1 + 3$
$y = {}^-4 + 3$ $\qquad\qquad$ $y = 0 + 3$ $\qquad\qquad$ $y = 2 + 3$
$y = {}^-1$ $\qquad\qquad\quad$ $y = 3$ $\qquad\qquad\qquad$ $y = 5$

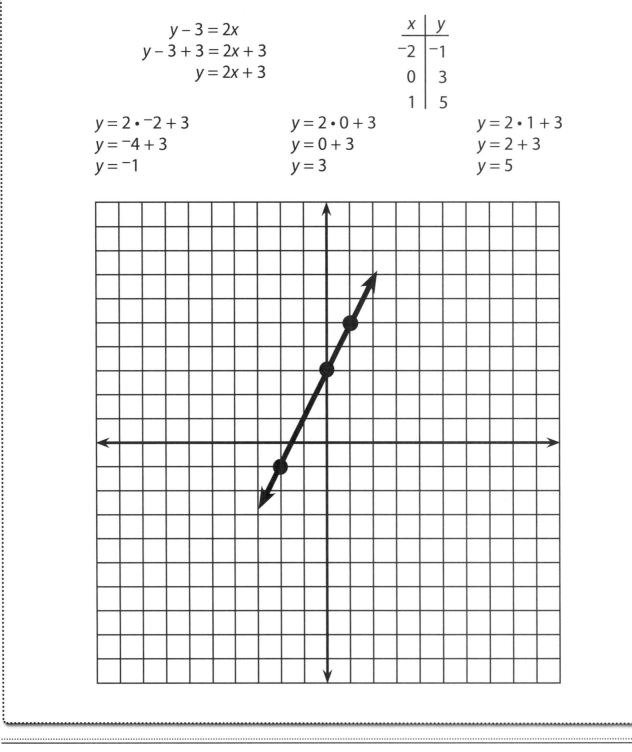

 CD-104316 • © Carson-Dellosa

Name _____ Date _____

Graphing

Graphing Linear Equations

Graph each equation by plotting points.

1. $x + y = 4$

x	y
4	
5	
6	

2. $y = 3 - x$

x	y
5	
−2	
0	

3. $4x + y = 6$

x	y
0	
1	
2	

4. $y = 2x - 7$

x	y
3	
4	
5	

5. $y = x + 3$

x	y
2	
0	
−3	

6. $y = 9 - x$

x	y
0	
4	
3	

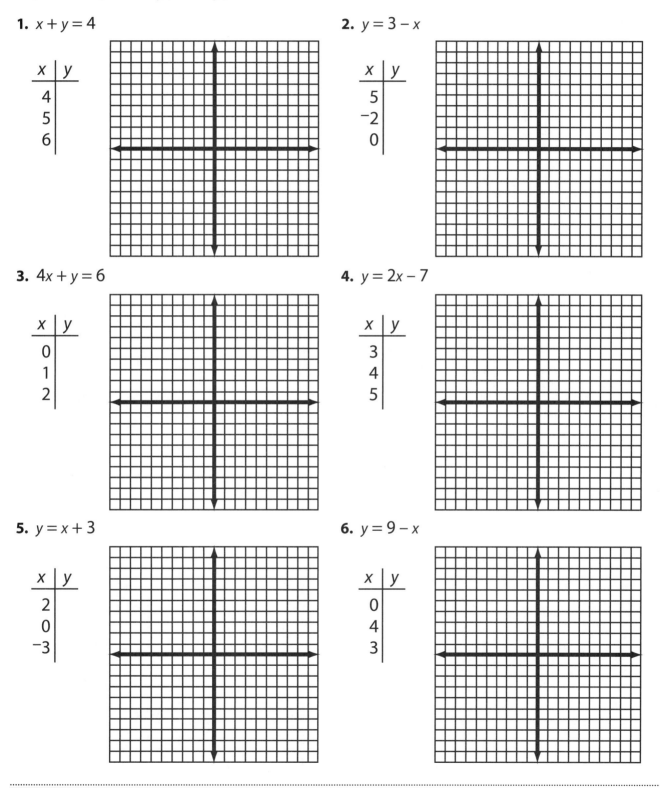

Graphing

Graphing Linear Equations

Graph each equation by plotting points.

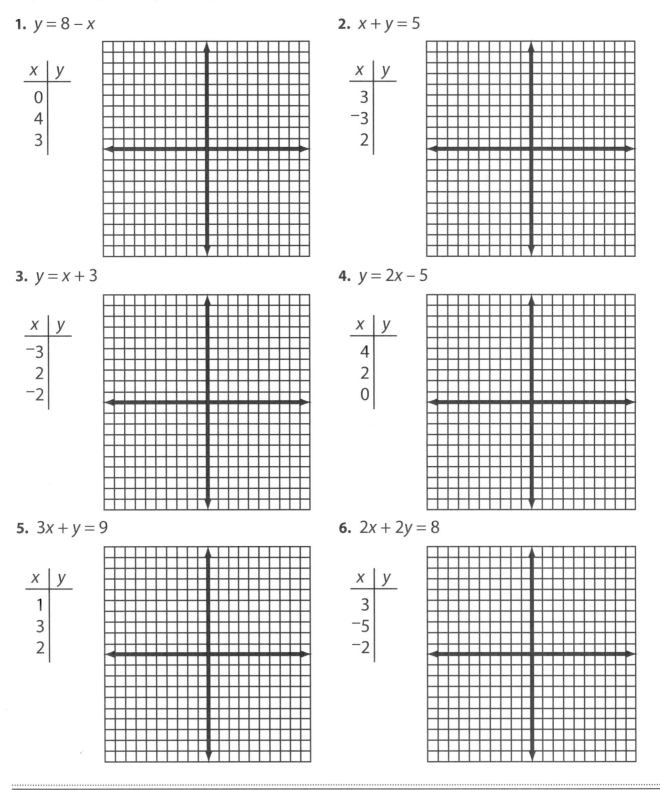

1. $y = 8 - x$

x	y
0	
4	
3	

2. $x + y = 5$

x	y
3	
−3	
2	

3. $y = x + 3$

x	y
−3	
2	
−2	

4. $y = 2x - 5$

x	y
4	
2	
0	

5. $3x + y = 9$

x	y
1	
3	
2	

6. $2x + 2y = 8$

x	y
3	
−5	
−2	

   CD-104316 • © Carson-Dellosa

Name _____ Date _____

Graphing

Slope-Intercept Form

The slope (*m*) of a line containing two points, P_1 and P_2, whose coordinates are (x_1, y_1) and (x_2, y_2), is given by:

$$\text{Slope} = m = \frac{y_2 - y_1}{x_2 - x_1}, x_2 \neq x_1$$

To find the **y-intercept (b)**, let $x = 0$.

$8x - 2y = {}^-6$
$y = 4x + 3$
$m = \dfrac{4}{1} \begin{matrix}(\text{up}) \\ (\text{to right})\end{matrix}$
$b = 3$

Solve for *y*, state the *m* and *b*, and graph.

1. $4x - 2y = {}^-12$

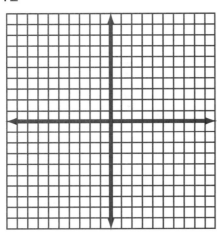

2. $2x + 2y + 4 = 0$

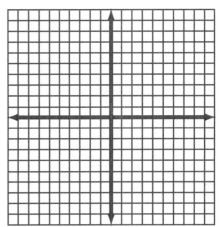

3. $y - 3x = 6$

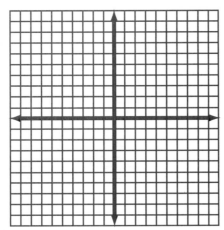

4. $5x + y = {}^-10$

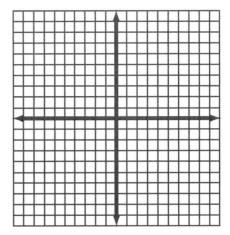

Name _____ Date _____

Graphing

Slope-Intercept Form

Solve for *y*, state the *m* and *b*, and graph.

1. $2x + 3y = 9$

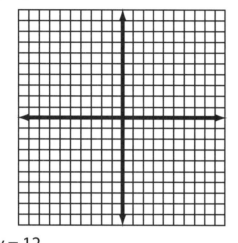

2. $x - 3y + 9 = 0$

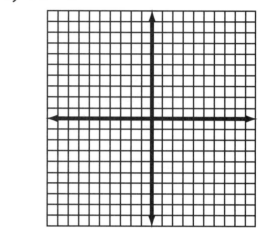

3. $6x + 2y = 12$

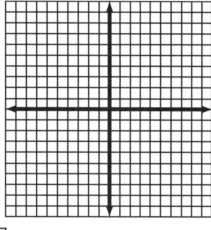

4. $y = 2x - 4$

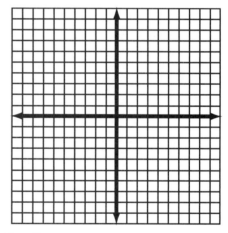

5. $5x - y = 7$

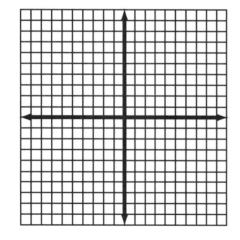

6. $x - 3y + 6 = 0$

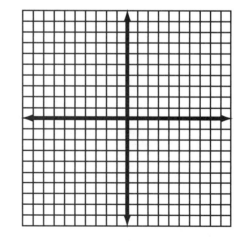

CD-104316 • © Carson-Dellosa

Graphing

Slope-Intercept Form

Solve for *y*, state the *m* and *b*, and graph.

1. $6x - 4y + 8 = 0$

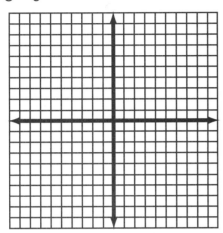

2. $y = 4x - 2$

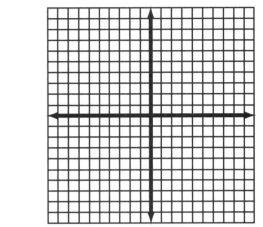

3. $5x + 3y = 18$

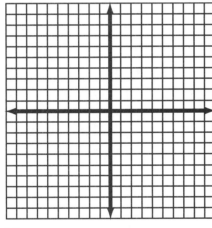

4. $2y = 4x - 16$

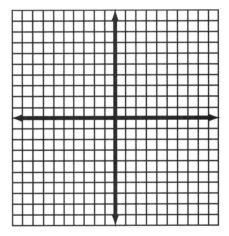

5. $3x - 3y = 12$

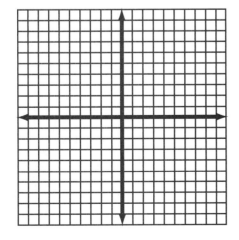

6. $y = 2x + 1$

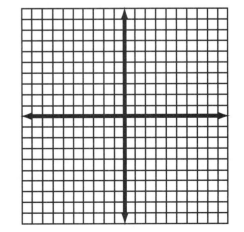

Name _____ Date _____

Graphing

X- and *Y*-Intercepts

To find the *x*-intercept, let $y = 0$. To find the *y*-intercept, let $x = 0$. Graph $4x - y = 4$ by using the *x*- and *y*-intercepts.

x-intercept	**y-intercept**
$2x - y = 2$	$2x - y = 2$
$2x - 0 = 2$	$2(0) - y = 2$
$2x = 2$	$^-y = 2$
$x = 1$	$y = ^-2$
$(1, 0)$	$(0, -2)$

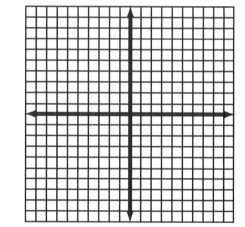

Find the *x*- and *y*-intercepts and graph.

1. $3x - 9y = 18$

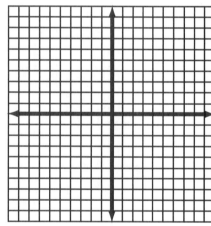

2. $4x + 2y = ^-8$

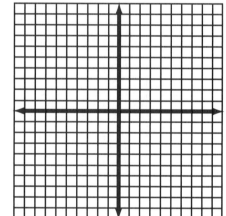

3. $2x + 4y = 20$

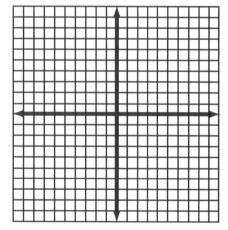

4. $x + 5y = 10$

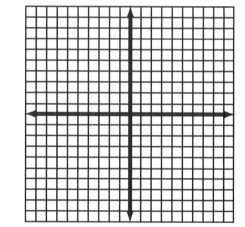

CD-104316 • © Carson-Dellosa

X- and *Y*-Intercepts

Writing an Equation of a Line

> **Slope-intercept Form of a Straight Line**
> For all equations of the form $y = mx + b$, m is the slope of the line.
> The y-intercept is $(0, b)$.
> This equation, $y = mx + b$, is the **slope-intercept of a straight line**.
> When the equation is in the form $Ax + By = C$, solve the equation for y.
> Once you have solved for y, follow the same procedure used for an
> equation in the form $y = mx + b$.

Write each equation below in slope-intercept form.

1. $4y - 2x = 32$

2. $^-4x + y = 8$

3. $3y = 2x + 12$

4. $^-7x + 3y + 21 = 0$

5. $2y - x = 6$

6. $y - 6 = 2x$

7. $y - x + 5 = 0$

8. $4y + 20 = 5x$

Find the equation of a line using the slope-intercept form: $y = mx + b$.

1. $m = ^-\dfrac{7}{5}$ $b = ^-2$

2. $m = \dfrac{3}{4}$ $b = \dfrac{2}{3}$

3. $m = \dfrac{3}{7}$ $b = \dfrac{1}{3}$

4. $m = \dfrac{3}{5}$ $b = \dfrac{1}{5}$

5. $m = ^-4$ $b = \dfrac{3}{4}$

6. $m = 0$ $b = \dfrac{2}{5}$

7. $m = \dfrac{1}{4}$ $b = \dfrac{2}{3}$

X- **and** *Y-***Intercepts**

Writing an Equation of a Line

Slope-Intercept Formula
$y = mx + b$
m: slope
b: *y*-intercept containing
coordinate points (*o*, *b*)

$m = 4$, passing through points (1, 2)
Using this information, {$m = 4, x = 1, y = 2$}.
Substitute into $y = mx + b$ to find *b*.
$$2 = (4)(1) + b \longrightarrow 2 = 4 + b$$
$$\longrightarrow 2 - 4 = 4 - 4 + b \longrightarrow {}^{-}2 = b$$
With the information $m = 4, b = {}^{-}2$, write
the equation as $y = 4x - 2$.

Find the equation of the line with the given slope passing through the indicated point (*P*).

1. $m = 3, P\,({}^{-}2, {}^{-}6)$

  $b =$

  Equation _____

2. $m = 1, P\,({}^{-}4, 3)$

  $b =$

  Equation _____

3. $m = 0, P\,(3, 5)$

  $b =$

  Equation _____

4. $m = 3, P\,(5, 7)$

  $b =$

  Equation _____

5. $m = {}^{-}7, P\,({}^{-}7, {}^{-}7)$

  $b =$

  Equation _____

6. $m = 4, P\,(2, {}^{-}6)$

  $b =$

  Equation _____

7. $m = 4, P\,(2, 4)$

  $b =$

  Equation _____

8. $m = {}^{-}5, P\,(6, {}^{-}1)$

  $b =$

  Equation _____

9. $m = 2, P\,({}^{-}1, 1)$

  $b =$

  Equation _____

10. $m = 2, P\,({}^{-}1, {}^{-}6)$

  $b =$

  Equation _____

11. $m = {}^{-}2, P\,(4, 5)$

  $b =$

  Equation _____

12. $m = {}^{-}6, P\,(2, 6)$

  $b =$

  Equation _____

CD-104316 • © Carson-Dellosa

Name _____ Date _____

X- and *Y*-Intercepts

Graphing Linear Inequalities

Graph: $y > 2x + 3$

1. Graph the line $y = 2x + 3$. $m = \frac{2}{1}$ $b = 3$

2. If > or <, connect points with dotted line 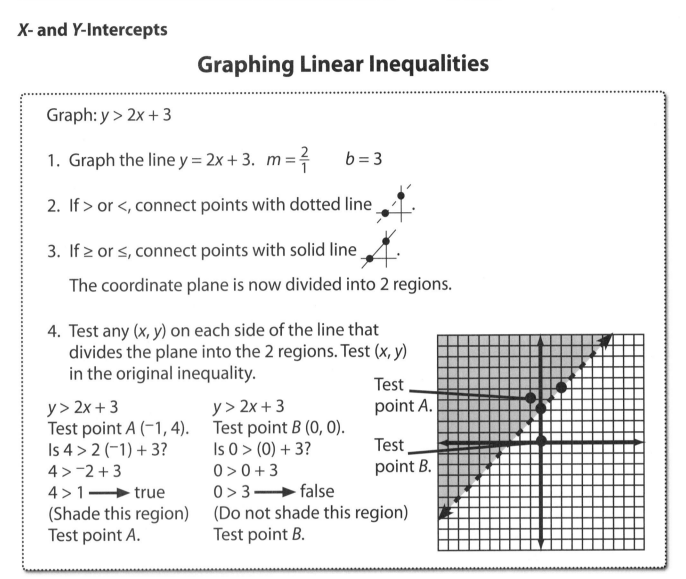.

3. If ≥ or ≤, connect points with solid line.

   The coordinate plane is now divided into 2 regions.

4. Test any (x, y) on each side of the line that divides the plane into the 2 regions. Test (x, y) in the original inequality.

$y > 2x + 3$	$y > 2x + 3$
Test point A (⁻1, 4).	Test point B (0, 0).
Is $4 > 2\,(^{-}1) + 3$?	Is $0 > (0) + 3$?
$4 > ^{-}2 + 3$	$0 > 0 + 3$
$4 > 1 \longrightarrow$ true	$0 > 3 \longrightarrow$ false
(Shade this region)	(Do not shade this region)
Test point A.	Test point B.

Test point A.

Test point B.

Graph the solution set.

1. $x + 4y > 8$

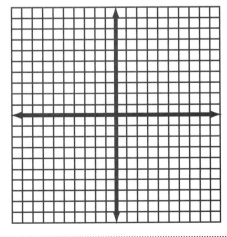

2. $^{-}2x + 2y > 10$

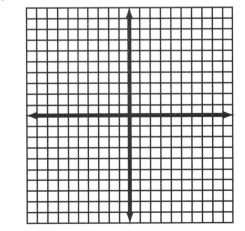

X- and *Y*-Intercepts

Graphing Linear Inequalities

Graph the solution set.

1. $3x + 2y \geq 6$

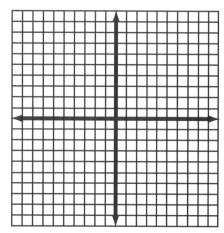

2. $2x + y < 4$

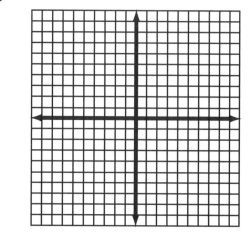

3. $6x - 3y > 15$

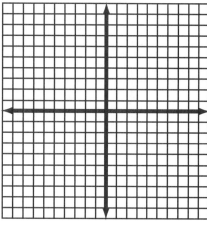

4. $2x + 3y \geq 6$

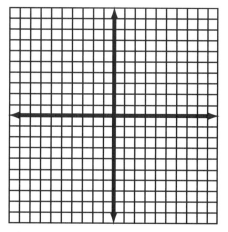

5. $3x - 4y \leq 12$

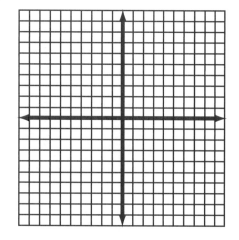

6. $4x + 2y < 6$

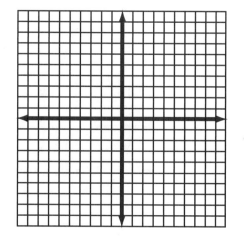

CD-104316 • © Carson-Dellosa

Name _____   Date _____

X- and Y-Intercepts

Graphing Linear Inequalities

Graph the solution set.

1. $x + 2y < 0$

2. $5x - 2y \leq 10$

3. $6x - 3y > 18$

4. $2x - 5y < 10$

5. $5x + 5y < 15$

6. $y + 6 > 0$

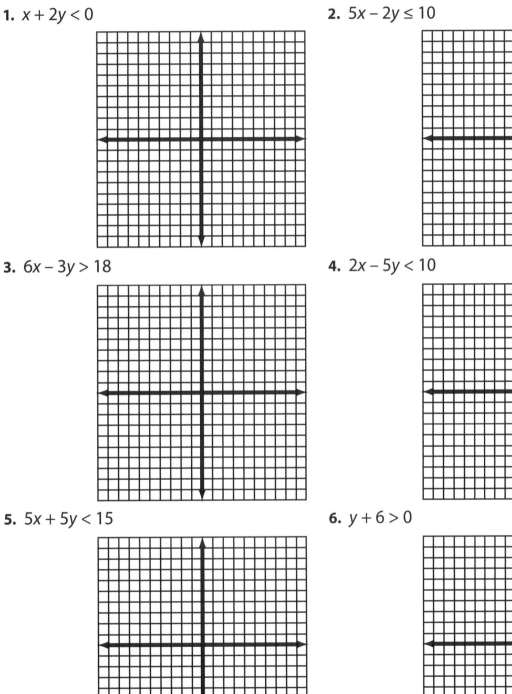

Name _____   Date _____

Solving Systems of Linear Equations by Graphing

When two or more equations are considered together, it is called a **system of equations**. The following example is a system of two linear equations in two variables.

$x + 2y = 4$
$2x + y = {}^-1$

The graphs of these equations are straight lines.

An ordered pair that is a solution of each equation of the system is a **solution of the system of equations in two variables**.

The solution of a system of linear equations can be found by graphing the lines of the system. The solution of the system of equations is the point where the lines of the ordered pair intersect.

Solve by graphing:

$x + 2y = 4$
$2x + y = {}^-1$

Graph each line and find the point of intersection.

The solution is $({}^-2, 3)$ because the ordered pair lies on each line.

Solve by graphing.

1. $x + y = 7$
   $3x - y = {}^-3$

2. $x + y = 4$
   $x - y = 6$

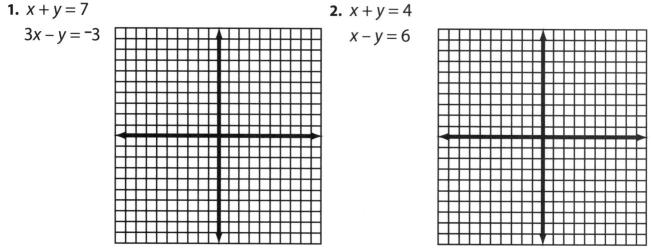

X- and Y-Intercepts

Solving Systems of Linear Equations by Graphing

Solve by graphing.

1. $3x - 4y = 12$
   $2x + 4y = {}^-12$

2. $4x - 2y = 8$
   $y = 3$

3. $x - y = 1$
   $x + 2y = 10$

4. $x = 5$
   $y = {}^-1$

5. $y = 2x + 4$
   $y = x + 6$

6. $x - y = {}^-4$
   $3x - y = {}^-12$

7. $x + y = 3$
   $x - y = 5$

8. $x = 4$
   $6x - 2y = 4$

***X*- and *Y*-Intercepts**

Solving Systems of Linear Equations by Graphing

Solve by graphing.

1. $y = x - 3$
   $x = 2y + 6$

2. $^-2x + y = 0$
   $2x + 4y = ^-8$

3. $y = 3x + 5$
   $y = 1 - x$

4. $y = x - 5$
   $y + 2x = 1$

5. $x - 4y = 2$
   $x + 2y = 8$

6. $x + y = 6$
   $3x - y = 2$

7. $2x + y = 6$
   $3x + y = 12$

8. $y = x + 3$
   $2y = 3x + 1$

CD-104316 • © Carson-Dellosa

X- and Y-Intercepts

Solving Systems of Linear Equations by Addition Method

$$2x + 3y = 7$$
$$x - y = {}^-1$$
$$3x = 6$$
$$\frac{3x}{3} = \frac{6}{3}$$
$$\mathbf{x = 2}$$
Substitute 2 for x
in $2x + 3y = 7$. ——

$$2x + 3y = 7$$
$$2(2) + 3y = 7$$
$$4 + 3y = 7$$
$$3y = 3$$
$$\mathbf{y = 1}$$

answer (2, 1)

Solve.

1. $2x - 5 = y$
$x - 7 = {}^-y$

2. $x + 4y = 2$
${}^-x + y = 8$

3. $y = 2x - 2$
${}^-y = x$

4. $3x + y = 8$
$3x - y = 4$

5. $2x - y = 6$
$3x + y = 4$

6. $y = 5x + 1$
$2y = {}^-5x + 2$

7. $x + y = 7$
$x - y = 3$

8. $3x + y = 5$
$x - y = 7$

9. $3x - 4y = 14$
$x + 4y = 2$

10. $5x - 3y = {}^-1$
$4x + 3y = 10$

11. $8x - 3y = 1$
${}^-8x + 5y = 9$

12. $3y - 4x = 5$
$y + 4x = 7$

13. $2x - 2y = 14$
$x + 2y = 1$

14. $2x - 7y = 4$
${}^-x + 7y = {}^-9$

X- and Y-Intercepts

Solving Systems of Linear Equations by Multiplication with Addition Method

1. Solve the following.
   $6x + 5y = 6$
   $6x - 3y = 6$

3. $\left.\begin{array}{l} 6x + 5y = \ \ 6 \\ \underline{^-6x + 3y = ^-6} \\ \hphantom{^-6x + 3}8y = 0 \\ \hphantom{^-6x + 3}y = 0 \end{array}\right\}$ Use the addition method.

2. $\left.\begin{array}{l} \hphantom{(^-1)(}6x + 5y = 6 \\ (^-1)(6x - 3y = 6) \end{array}\right\}$ Multiply to create the additive inverse.

4. $\left.\begin{array}{l} 6x + 5y = 6 \\ 6x + 5(0) = 6 \\ 6x = 6 \\ x = 1 \end{array}\right\}$ Substitute.

Solve the following.

1. $3x + 8y = 8$
   $2x + y = 1$

2. $3x - 4y = 4$
   $x - y = 1$

3. $4x - 4y = 16$
   $2x + 2y = 4$

4. $2x - 5y = 21$
   $x + y = 7$

5. $4x + 8y = 20$
   $x - y = 2$

6. $6x + 4y = ^-22$
   $3x + 6y = ^-7$

7. $2x + y = 3$
   $x + 3y = 4$

8. $3x + 3y = ^-3$
   $x - y = ^-5$

9. $4x + 2y = 10$
   $x + 2y = 1$

10. $3x + 5y = ^-8$
    $x + 7y = ^-8$

 CD-104316 • © Carson-Dellosa

X- and *Y*-Intercepts

Solving Systems of Linear Equations by Substitution

$4x + 4y = 12$
$3x + y = 9 \longrightarrow y = 9 - 3x$
$4x + 4(9 - 3x) = 12$
$4x + 36 - 12x = 12$
$36 - 8x = 12$
$^-8x = ^-24$
$x = 3$
Solution $(3, 0)$

Solve.

1. $y = 3 - 2x$
$y = 2 - 3x$

2. $x + y = 5$
$x = y + 7$

3. $x - y = 1$
$2x + y = 8$

4. $3x - y = 9$
$y = x + 5$

5. $3x + 4y = 26$
$^-2x + y = 1$

6. $y = 2x + 3$
$y = 4x + 4$

7. $2x + 7y = 8$
$x + 5y = 7$

8. $y = 4x + 4$
$y = 2x + 8$

9. $x + 3y = 17$
$2x + 3y = 22$

10. $4x - 7y = 9$
$y = x - 3$

11. $8x - 5y = 9$
$y = 2x - 4$

12. $2x + 4y = ^-2$
$3x + y = 7$

13. $3x + y = 5$
$2x + 3y = 8$

14. $2x + 6y = 24$
$x - 4y = ^-2$

Name _____   Date _____

Radicals

Simplifying Radicals

$$\sqrt{49x^4y^8} = 7\sqrt{x^4y^8} = 7x^2y^4$$

Simplify.

1. $\sqrt{x^2y^{10}} =$

2. $\sqrt{27x^8} =$

3. $\sqrt{x^{16}} =$

4. $\sqrt{125b^{15}} =$

5. $\sqrt{x^{14}y^6} =$

6. $\sqrt{169y^{12}} =$

7. $\sqrt{16x^4} =$

8. $\sqrt{8x^3} =$

9. $\sqrt{81x^6} =$

10. $\sqrt{25x^6} =$

11. $\sqrt{x^9y^9} =$

12. $\sqrt{a^{12}} =$

13. $\sqrt{9a^4b^8} =$

14. $\sqrt{54x^8} =$

15. $\sqrt{49x^4y^2} =$

16. $\sqrt{x^8} =$

17. $\sqrt{8x^9} =$

18. $\sqrt{81x^9y^{12}} =$

19. $\sqrt{8x^4} =$

20. $\sqrt{x^3y^9} =$

 CD-104316 • © Carson-Dellosa

Radicals

Simplifying Radicals

$$\sqrt{64x^2y^4} = 8\sqrt{x^2y^4} = 8xy^2$$

Simplify.

1. $\sqrt{81x^6} =$

2. $\sqrt{6x^2} =$

3. $\sqrt{9x^3} =$

4. $\sqrt{12y^5} =$

5. $\sqrt{9x^4} =$

6. $\sqrt{81x^6} =$

7. $\sqrt{12x^2y^4} =$

8. $\sqrt{6x^9} =$

9. $\sqrt{21x^2} =$

10. $\sqrt{x^3} =$

11. $\sqrt{4x^5y^2} =$

12. $\sqrt{64a^3b^6} =$

13. $\sqrt{4x^7} =$

14. $\sqrt{9x^5y^{16}} =$

15. $\sqrt{18x^3y^4} =$

16. $\sqrt{9x^3y^4} =$

17. $\sqrt{12x^4y^8} =$

18. $\sqrt{8x^4} =$

19. $\sqrt{27x^7} =$

20. $\sqrt{9x^6} =$

Radicals

Multiplying Radicals

$$\sqrt{3a} \cdot \sqrt{4a} = \sqrt{12a^2} = \sqrt{3} \cdot 4 \cdot a^2 = 2a\sqrt{3}$$

Simplify.

1. $\sqrt{x^2y^4} \cdot 2\sqrt{xy} =$

2. $\sqrt{9} \cdot \sqrt{32} =$

3. $3\sqrt{5} \cdot 2\sqrt{4} =$

4. $4\sqrt{9x^3} \cdot 3\sqrt{4x} =$

5. $2\sqrt{4x^3y} \cdot y\sqrt{x^5y^7} =$

6. $x\sqrt{5x^3y} \cdot x\sqrt{5x^2y} =$

7. $2\sqrt{9x^2} \cdot 2\sqrt{4x^2} =$

8. $6\sqrt{9xy} \cdot 4\sqrt{2xy} =$

9. $2\sqrt{4x^3y} \cdot 3\sqrt{3a^2b^2} =$

10. $5\sqrt{2x^6y} \cdot 3\sqrt{3x^3y^5} =$

11. $4\sqrt{8a^6b} \cdot 4\sqrt{8a^4b^4} =$

12. $3\sqrt{2x^3} \cdot 3\sqrt{3x^2y^2} =$

13. $5\sqrt{4a} \cdot 2\sqrt{6a} =$

14. $x\sqrt{3x} \cdot x\sqrt{3x^3} =$

15. $\sqrt{2x^4} \cdot \sqrt{10x^2y^2} =$

16. $3\sqrt{4x^3y} \cdot 4\sqrt{5x^5y^7} =$

17. $x\sqrt{81} \cdot y\sqrt{36} =$

18. $4\sqrt{3x} \cdot 4\sqrt{4x} =$

19. $3\sqrt{8a} \cdot 8\sqrt{3a^3} =$

20. $2\sqrt{2a^6} \cdot 5\sqrt{3a^3b^5} =$

CD-104316 • © Carson-Dellosa

Radicals

Dividing Radicals

$$\sqrt{\frac{18}{2}} = \sqrt{9} = 3 \qquad\qquad \sqrt{\frac{9}{25}} = \frac{\sqrt{9}}{\sqrt{25}} = \frac{3}{5}$$

Simplify.

1. $\sqrt{\dfrac{36}{9}} =$

2. $\sqrt{\dfrac{27x}{3x}} =$

3. $\sqrt{\dfrac{x^2}{25}} =$

4. $\sqrt{\dfrac{8x^3}{2x}} =$

5. $\sqrt{\dfrac{18x^3}{2x}} =$

6. $\sqrt{\dfrac{9}{64}} =$

7. $\sqrt{\dfrac{27x^2}{3}} =$

8. $\sqrt{\dfrac{50x^2}{2}} =$

9. $\sqrt{\dfrac{49x^2}{25x^3}} =$

10. $\sqrt{\dfrac{12x^2}{60}} =$

11. $\sqrt{\dfrac{4x^3y}{4xy^3}} =$

12. $\sqrt{\dfrac{3x^4y^5}{x^3y^2}} =$

13. $\sqrt{\dfrac{2x^2}{18x^4}} =$

14. $\sqrt{\dfrac{3x^7}{108y^2}} =$

Radicals

Adding and Subtracting Radical Expressions

$$2\sqrt{y} + 3\sqrt{y} + \sqrt{y} = 6\sqrt{y} \qquad \sqrt{4x} + 3\sqrt{x} = 2\sqrt{x} + 3\sqrt{x} = 5\sqrt{x}$$

Simplify.

1. $3\sqrt{x^3} - 4\sqrt{x^3} =$

2. $3\sqrt{2y} + 2\sqrt{2y} =$

3. $2\sqrt{y} - 4\sqrt{y} =$

4. $3y\sqrt{2y} - y\sqrt{2y} =$

5. $x\sqrt{27} + x\sqrt{12} =$

6. $3\sqrt{6x} + 5\sqrt{6x} =$

7. $4\sqrt{2x^3} + 3\sqrt{2x^3} =$

8. $2\sqrt{50} - 4\sqrt{8} - 3\sqrt{72} =$

9. $4\sqrt{y^3} - 2\sqrt{y^3} =$

10. $3\sqrt{x^3} + 3\sqrt{x^2} =$

11. $y\sqrt{y^4} - 2y\sqrt{y^4} =$

12. $x\sqrt{6x} + x\sqrt{24x} =$

13. $4x\sqrt{x^3} + 2x\sqrt{x^3} =$

14. $5\sqrt{24y} + \sqrt{54y} =$

15. $4\sqrt{x} - 2\sqrt{x} - 3\sqrt{x} + 5\sqrt{x} =$

16. $3\sqrt{4x^2y} - 8y\sqrt{y} =$

17. $3\sqrt{9x^2y^2} + 2\sqrt{9x^2y^2} =$

18. $6\sqrt{6y} + 7\sqrt{6y} + 2\sqrt{6y} =$

19. $3x\sqrt{4x^3y^2} - 5\sqrt{x^3y^2} =$

20. $2\sqrt{4x} + 3\sqrt{2x} - 4\sqrt{2x} + 4\sqrt{4x} =$

CD-104316 • © Carson-Dellosa

Factoring

Solving Equations by Taking Square Roots

$$x^2 = 49$$
$$\sqrt{x^2} = \sqrt{49}$$ The solutions are 7 and $^-$7.
$$x = \pm\, 7$$

Solve by taking square roots.

1. $x^2 = 9$ **2.** $x^2 - 81 = 0$

3. $x^2 = 144$ **4.** $x^2 = 100$

5. $a^2 = 196$ **6.** $x^2 - 49 = 0$

7. $5x^2 - 125 = 0$ **8.** $x^2 - 121 = 0$

9. $x^2 - 64 = 0$ **10.** $x^2 - 361 = 0$

11. $x^2 + 81 = 162$ **12.** $3x^2 - 432 = 0$

13. $3x^2 - 108 = 0$ **14.** $a^2 - 169 = 0$

15. $2x^2 - 128 = 0$ **16.** $2a^2 - 242 = 0$

17. $x^2 - 225 = 0$ **18.** $3x^2 - 147 = 0$

19. $x^2 - 25 = 0$ **20.** $4x^2 - 16 = 0$

Factoring

Solving Quadratic Equations by Factoring

$x^2 - 8x = {}^-16$ $x - 4 = 0$
$x^2 - 8x + 16 = 0$ $x = 4$
$(x - 4)(x - 4) = 0$ The solution is 4.

Solve by factoring.

1. $y^2 + 9y = 0$

2. $x - 16 = x(x - 7)$

3. $x - 6 = x(x - 4)$

4. $x^2 + 7x = 0$

5. $x^2 - 4x = 0$

6. $x + 8 = x(x + 3)$

7. $y^2 - y - 6 = 0$

8. $a^2 - 36 = 0$

9. $y^2 + 15 = 8y$

10. $a^2 - 7a = {}^-12$

11. $y^2 + 36y = 0$

12. $3u^2 - 12u - 15 = 0$

13. $y^2 - 8y + 12 = 0$

14. $5a^2 + 25a = 0$

15. $6x^2 + 18x = 0$

16. $2x^2 + x = 6$

17. $x^2 - 5x - 6 = 0$

18. $4x^2 + 16x = 0$

19. $3x^2 - 9x = 0$

20. $y^2 + 5y - 6 = 0$

                    CD-104316 • © Carson-Dellosa

Factoring

Solving Quadratic Equations by Factoring

Solve by factoring.

1. $a^2 - 8a = 0$

2. $x^2 = 3x + 4$

3. $4a^2 + 15a - 4 = 0$

4. $x^2 - x - 6 = 0$

5. $3x^2 - 13x + 4 = 0$

6. $6x^2 = 23x + 18$

7. $x^2 + 7x + 12 = 0$

8. $x^2 + 5x - 6 = 0$

9. $x^2 = 6x + 7$

10. $x^2 = 10x - 25$

11. $x^2 + 3x - 10 = 0$

12. $x^2 - 6x + 9 = 0$

13. $y^2 - 3y + 2 = 0$

14. $2x^2 - 9x + 9 = 0$

15. $r^2 - 15r = 16$

16. $x^2 + 7x + 10 = 0$

17. $3x^2 - 2x - 8 = 0$

18. $2a^2 + 4a - 6 = 0$

19. $x^2 + 3x - 4 = 0$

20. $4a^2 + 9a + 2 = 0$

21. $9x^2 = 18x + 0$

22. $2x^2 = 9x + 5$

Radicals

Solving Quadratic Equations by Taking Square Roots

$$x^2 = 36$$
$$\sqrt{x^2} = \sqrt{36}$$ The solutions are 6 and $^-6$.
$$x = \pm 6$$

Solve by taking square roots.

1. $a^2 = 9$ **2.** $x^2 = 81$

3. $x^2 = 49$ **4.** $x^2 = 36$

5. $x^2 - 36 = 0$ **6.** $x^2 - 81 = 0$

7. $x^2 - 16 = 0$ **8.** $a^2 - 4 = 0$

9. $3x^2 - 75 = 0$ **10.** $3x^2 - 27 = 0$

11. $(x + 2)^2 = 36$ **12.** $9a^2 - 81 = 0$

13. $(x + 1)^2 = 36$ **14.** $3x^2 - 108 = 0$

15. $6x^2 - 24 = 0$ **16.** $4(x + 2)^2 = 64$

17. $4(x - 3)^2 = 16$ **18.** $3a^2 - 27 = 0$

19. $3(x + 3)^2 = 27$ **20.** $(x + 2)^2 = 4$

Logical Reasoning and Application
Probability Experiment—Directional Page

Directional Page

Review all terms given on these worksheets and follow the directions below. Answer all questions with your partner.

1. Designate one partner "A" and one partner "B."

2. On your worksheet, calculate the theoretical probability for tossing a fair coin and getting "heads" (H) and "tails" (T). Record these probabilities on the worksheet as directed, changing all fractions to decimals for ease of comparison.

3. Answer questions 1, 2, and 3 on your worksheet now.

4. Get one fair coin from your teacher.

5. "A" flips the coin 10 times while "B" records each outcome as "H" for heads or "T" for tails.

6. For the next 10 coin flips, "B" flips the coin while "A" records the outcomes.

7. Continue alternating tasks every 10 coin tosses until you have completed 100 coin tosses.

8. Analyze this experimental data based on the theoretical probability you calculated earlier.

9. Answer questions 4 and 5 on the worksheets.

10. There should be a grid on the board to hold all of the experimental data from each cooperative group. Partner "A" should then write the group's experimental data on the board. A class discussion of combined data should follow.

11. After the class discussion of the combined data, refine your answer to question 5 on worksheet. Write at least 2 sentences comparing class data to your own experimental data.

Extension Activity: Toss the coin 25, 50, or 100 more times and record the results.
*** Teacher's note – Each group should receive the following:
1 Directional sheet
1 Terminology and calculations sheet
1 Tally sheet
1 Question sheet
1 Fair coin (penny)

Logical Reasoning and Application
Probability Experiment

Terminology and Calculations Page

Probability is the chance that a given event will occur, expressed mathematically as a ratio from 0 (no chance) to 1 (absolutely certain).

Sample Space is the set of all possible outcomes of an event.

Outcomes represent each member of the sample space.

Theoretical Probability is the ratio of the number of possible outcomes of a given event to the total number of outcomes in the sample space. In other words, theoretical probability is which outcomes will probably occur, given the variables of the situation. We will denote this as P(H) and P(T), for the theoretical probability of "heads" and "tails," respectively.

Sample Space: Fair Coin {_____}

Calculate:

$$P(H) = \{\frac{\text{no. of times H occurs in sample space}}{\text{total no. of outcomes in sample space}}\} = 0.\underline{\hphantom{xx}}$$

$$P(T) = \{\frac{\text{no. of times T occurs in sample space}}{\text{total no. of outcomes in sample space}}\} = 0.\underline{\hphantom{xx}}$$

Experimental Probability is the ratio of the frequency of an event to the number of random experiments conducted. We will denote this as P(H) and P(T), for the theoretical probability of "heads" and "tails," respectively.

Flip a coin 50 times. Record _H_ for heads and _T_ for tails after each flip. Use your experimental data to calculate.

Sample Space: 10 flips {   }

25 Flips {   }

50 Flips {   }

$$P(H) = \{\frac{\text{No. of heads}}{10}\} = \frac{}{10} = 0.\underline{\hphantom{xx}} \qquad P(T) = \{\frac{\text{No. of tails}}{10}\} = \frac{}{10} = 0.\underline{\hphantom{xx}}$$

$$P(H) = \{\frac{\text{No. of heads}}{25}\} = \frac{}{25} = 0.\underline{\hphantom{xx}} \qquad P(T) = \{\frac{\text{No. of tails}}{25}\} = \frac{}{25} = 0.\underline{\hphantom{xx}}$$

$$P(H) = \{\frac{\text{No. of heads}}{50}\} = \frac{}{50} = 0.\underline{\hphantom{xx}} \qquad P(T) = \{\frac{\text{No of tails}}{50}\} = \frac{}{50} = 0.\underline{\hphantom{xx}}$$

Logical Reasoning and Application
Probability Experiment

Questions Page

As cooperative pairs, answer the following questions.

1. Explain in your own words the difference between theoretical and experimental probabilities.

2. Of what similar sounding word does *probability* remind you?

3. What predictions (conjectures) can you make about the results of your experiment based on the theoretical probability of tossing "heads" or "tails"? In other words, what do you think will happen when you toss a coin 10, 50, and 100 times and analyze the results?

4. Analyze the results of your experiment. Does your experimental probability confirm or contradict your original predictions about the likelihood of tossing a fair coin and getting "heads" or "tails"?

5. Make a statement about the relationship between experimental and theoretical probabilities of a given event based on your experiment.

Name _____   Date _____

Logical Reasoning and Application
Probability Experiment

Tally Sheet

Write *H* or *T* next to each number as the coin is flipped. Record the total number of *H*s or *T*s per 10 coin flips in the end column.

Key: H = Heads T = Tails										H	T
1	2	3	4	5	6	7	8	9	10		
11	12	13	14	15	16	17	18	19	20		
21	22	23	24	25	26	27	28	29	30		
31	32	33	34	35	36	37	38	39	40		
41	42	43	44	45	46	47	48	49	50		
51	52	53	54	55	56	57	58	59	60		
61	62	63	64	65	66	67	68	69	70		
71	72	73	74	75	76	77	78	79	80		
81	82	83	84	85	86	87	88	89	90		
91	92	93	94	95	96	97	98	99	100		

   CD-104316 • © Carson-Dellosa

Reproducible $\frac{1}{8}$-inch graph paper

Reproducible $\frac{1}{4}$-inch graph paper

CD-104316 • © Carson-Dellosa

Reproducible $\frac{1}{2}$-inch graph paper

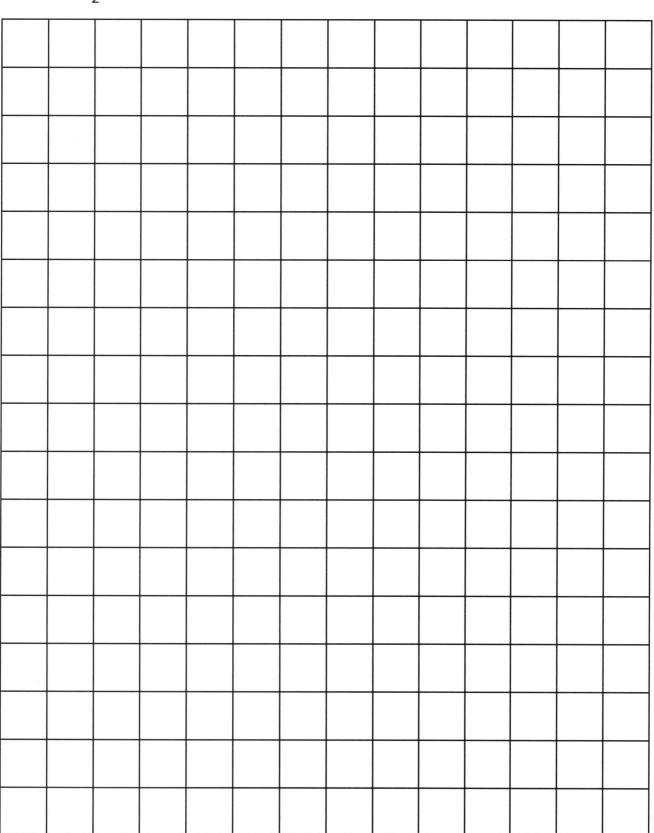

Name _____ Date _____

Operations with Real Numbers

Patterns

The French mathematician Blaise Pascal developed a triangular pattern to describe the coefficients for the expansion of $(a + b)^n$, for consecutive values of n in rows. This pattern is referred to as Pascal's triangle.

In the triangular formation below, note that $(a + b)^0 = 1$ and $(a + b)^1 = a + b$.

Part A. Fill in the blanks in Pascal's triangle to extend the pattern.

$n = 0$ 1

$n = 1$ 1   1

$n = 2$ 1   2   1

$n = 3$ 1   3   3   1

$n = 4$ 1   **4**   6   **4**   1

$n = 5$ **1**   **5**   **10**   10   **5**   **1**

$n = 6$ **1**   **6**   **15**   **20**   **15**   **6**   **1**

$n = 7$ **1**   **7**   **21**   **35**   **35**   **21**   **7**   **1**

$n = 8$ **1**   **8**   **28**   **56**   **70**   **56**   **28**   **8**   **1**

$n = 9$ **1**   **9**   **36**   **84**   **126**   **126**   **84**   **36**   **9**   **1**

$n = 10$ **1**   **10**   **45**   **120**   **210**   **252**   **210**   **120**   **45**   **10**   **1**

Part B. Use Pascal's triangle to find the coefficients of the expansion $(a + b)$.

1. $(a + b)^3 = \underline{1}a^3 + \underline{3}a^2b + \underline{3}ab^2 + \underline{1}b^3$

2. $(a + b)^6 = \underline{1}a^6 + \underline{6}a^5b + \underline{15}a^4b^2 + \underline{20}a^3b^3 + \underline{15}a^2b^4 + \underline{6}ab^5 + \underline{1}b^6$

3. $(a + b)^4 = \underline{1}a^4 + \underline{4}a^3b + \underline{6}a^2b^2 + \underline{4}ab^3 + \underline{1}b^4$

4. $(a + b)^7 = \underline{1}a^7 + \underline{7}a^6b + \underline{21}a^5b^2 + \underline{35}a^4b^3 + \underline{35}a^3b^4 + \underline{21}a^2b^5 + \underline{7}ab^6 + \underline{1}b^7$

CD-104316 • © Carson-Dellosa   5

Name _____ Date _____

Operations with Real Numbers

Patterns

Carefully study the patterns of numbers to complete each pattern.

1. 130, 120, 110, 100, **90**, **80**, **70**, **60**

2. 20, 200, 2,000, 20,000, **200,000**, **2,000,000**, **20,000,000**

3. 3, 6, 7, 14, 15, 30, 31, **62**, **63**, **126**, **127**

4. 1, 4, 9, 16, 25, **36**, **49**, **64**, **81**, **100**

5. 1, 6, 5, 10, 9, 14, 13, **18**, **17**, **22**, **21**

6. $\frac{1}{2}, \frac{2}{3}, \frac{3}{4}, \frac{4}{5}, \frac{5}{6}, \frac{6}{7},$ **$\frac{7}{8}$**, **$\frac{8}{9}$**, **$\frac{9}{10}$**, **$\frac{10}{11}$**

7. 17, 15, 25, 23, 33, 31, **41**, **39**, **49**, **47**

8. 7, 21, 63, 189, **567**, **1,701**, **5,103**, **15,309**

9. 800, 80, 8, 0.8, 0.08, **0.008**, **0.0008**, **0.00008**, **0.000008**

> **Challenge!** The following is a special pattern called the Fibonacci sequence. See if you can discover and complete this interesting pattern.

1, 1, 2, 3, 5, 8, 13, **21**, **34**, **55**, **89**, **144**

6   CD-104316 • © Carson-Dellosa

Name _____ Date _____

Operations with Real Numbers

Adding Real Numbers

$$^-7 + 6 = ^-1$$

Add.

1. $2.7 + (^-4.8) = $ **$^-2.1$**

2. $1.45 + 2.65 + (^-9.43) = $ **$^-5.33$**

3. $^-55 + (^-8) + (^-4) + 54 = $ **$^-13$**

4. $3.54 + 4.27 + 7.43 = $ **15.24**

5. $10 + 7 + (^-7) + (^-10) = $ **0**

6. $16 + 21 + (^-3) + 7 = $ **41**

7. $10 + 7 + (^-16) + 9 + (^-30) = $ **$^-20$**

8. $5.8 + 8.4 = $ **14.2**

9. $2.76 + (^-6.56) + (^-9.72) = $ **$^-13.52$**

10. $8 + (^-7) = $ **1**

11. $2\frac{3}{5} + 4\frac{3}{7} = $ **$7\frac{1}{35}$**

12. $^-8\frac{3}{5} + 3\frac{3}{7} = $ **$^-5\frac{6}{35}$**

13. $3\frac{5}{8} + (^-1\frac{2}{3}) + 2 = $ **$3\frac{23}{24}$**

14. $^-5\frac{3}{4} + (^-2\frac{3}{4}) + 8 = $ **$^-\frac{1}{2}$**

15. $7.3 + (3.9) = $ **11.2**

16. $^-21 + 12 + (^-1) + (^-17) = $ **$^-27$**

17. $7.867 + (^-5.329) = $ **2.538**

18. $^-2\frac{3}{5} + (^-5\frac{3}{7}) + 3 = $ **$^-5\frac{1}{35}$**

19. $3 + 12 + (^-13) + 36 = $ **38**

20. $^-3\frac{1}{6} + (^-9\frac{3}{12}) + 6 = $ **$^-6\frac{5}{12}$**

CD-104316 • © Carson-Dellosa   7

Name _____ Date _____

Operations with Real Numbers

Adding Real Numbers

$$^-6 + 3 = ^-3$$

Add.

1. $2\frac{3}{5} + (^-3\frac{2}{5}) + ^-6 =$ **$^-6\frac{4}{5}$**

2. $21 + 9 + (^-6) + 7 =$ **31**

3. $12 + (^-9) + 17 =$ **20**

4. $2.54 + ^-5.87 + ^-32.65 =$ **$^-35.98$**

5. $1 + ^-5 + (^-5) + 1 =$ **$^-8$**

6. $21 + 3 + (^-13) + 22 =$ **33**

7. $3 + (^-3) + 4 + (^-5) =$ **$^-1$**

8. $3.3 + (^-3.4) + 5.5 =$ **5.4**

9. $3.6 + (^-2.5) + ^-5.5 =$ **$^-4.4$**

10. $^-0.6 + (^-0.56) + 3 =$ **1.84**

11. $2 + 5 + ^-3 =$ **4**

12. $4.524 + 7.342 =$ **11.866**

13. $^-7\frac{2}{4} + 2\frac{3}{4} =$ **$^-4\frac{3}{4}$**

14. $34 + (^-13) + 18 + 0 + 34 =$ **73**

15. $8.43 + (^-10.98) + (^-3.23) =$ **$^-5.78$**

16. $2.54 + (^-5.21) + (^-6.34) =$ **$^-9.01$**

17. $^-2\frac{1}{3} + (^-5\frac{7}{10}) + (^-7) =$ **$^-15\frac{1}{30}$**

18. $^-1\frac{2}{3} + (^-3\frac{3}{5}) + 4 =$ **$^-1\frac{4}{15}$**

19. $2\frac{1}{2} + 6\frac{1}{2} =$ **9**

20. $4\frac{3}{5} + (^-3\frac{2}{5}) + (^-8) =$ **$^-6\frac{4}{5}$**

Name _____ Date _____

Operations with Real Numbers

Subtracting Real Numbers

$$10 - (^-4) = 10 + 4 = 14$$

Subtract.

1. $9 - (^-32) =$ **41**

2. $^-99 - (^-42) =$ **$^-57$**

3. $\frac{3}{5} - \frac{7}{8} =$ **$-\frac{11}{40}$**

4. $0 - 21 =$ **$^-21$**

5. $45 - 301 =$ **$^-256$**

6. $9.432 + 4.348 - 44.938 =$ **$^-31.158$**

7. $^-43 - 6 =$ **$^-49$**

8. $9 - (^-2) - 8 - 7 =$ **$^-4$**

9. $35 - 67 - 85 - 21 - 12 =$ **$^-150$**

10. $12 - 7 - (^-16) - 9 - (^-34) =$ **46**

11. $18 - (^-13) =$ **31**

12. $^-\frac{2}{5} - \frac{3}{4} - (^-\frac{4}{5}) =$ **$-\frac{7}{20}$**

13. $^-\frac{4}{7} - \frac{1}{3} - (\frac{2}{3}) =$ **$^-1\frac{4}{7}$**

14. $3.434 - 7.294 =$ **$^-3.86$**

15. $8 - 2.8 =$ **5.2**

16. $8 - (^-14) =$ **22**

17. $3.9 - 4.9 =$ **$^-1$**

18. $^-7 - (^-3) =$ **$^-4$**

19. $2.19 - 7.8 - 8.31 =$ **$^-13.92$**

20. $38 - 39 - (^-13) =$ **12**

Name _____ Date _____

Operations with Real Numbers

Subtracting Real Numbers

$$4 - (^-5) = 4 + 5 = 9$$

Subtract.

1. $^-9 - (^-5) =$ **$^-4$**

2. $321 - (^-34) =$ **355**

3. $\frac{2}{3} - \frac{4}{5} =$ **$-\frac{2}{15}$**

4. $4 - (^-8) =$ **12**

5. $5.34 - 9.9 - 3.65 =$ **$^-8.21$**

6. $^-19 - 8 =$ **$^-27$**

7. $245 - 32 - (^-36) =$ **249**

8. $44 - 35 - 34 - 32 =$ **$^-57$**

9. $8 - (^-5) - 7 - 9 =$ **$^-3$**

10. $43 - 88 - 35 - 21 =$ **$^-101$**

11. $121 - 45 =$ **76**

12. $^-45 - 5 =$ **$^-50$**

13. $^-\frac{2}{3} - \frac{1}{3} - (^-\frac{1}{3}) =$ **$-\frac{2}{3}$**

14. $^-\frac{4}{5} - \frac{1}{2} - \frac{2}{5} =$ **$^-1\frac{7}{10}$**

15. $4 - 12.9 =$ **$^-8.9$**

16. $7 - (^-33) =$ **40**

17. $3.4 - 7.4 =$ **$^-4$**

18. $2.456 - 4.345 - 5.457 =$ **$^-7.346$**

19. $23 - (^-21) =$ **44**

20. $4.346 - 0.4537 =$ **3.8923**

Name _____ Date _____

Operations with Real Numbers

Multiplying Real Numbers

$$(^-2)(^-3) = 6$$

Multiply.

1. $4 \cdot 9 =$ **36**

2. $^-4 \cdot 12 =$ **$^-48$**

3. $(^-\frac{5}{9})(8.8) =$ **$^-4.\overline{8}$**

4. $(^-3)(0) =$ **0**

5. $(^-3)(^-9) =$ **27**

6. $6(23) =$ **138**

7. $(12)(^-3)(4) =$ **$^-144$**

8. $(^-5)(^-5)(^-5) =$ **$^-125$**

9. $(5)(2)(^-1) =$ **$^-10$**

10. $(7)(^-9)(^-12) =$ **756**

11. $(^-\frac{2}{3})(^-1.6) =$ **$1.0\overline{6}$**

12. $^-7(^-7) =$ **49**

13. $(54.2)(^-3.55) =$ **$^-192.41$**

14. $(2.22)(^-1.11) =$ **$^-2.4642$**

15. $(7.44)(3.2)(4.3) =$ **102.3744**

16. $(2.4)(^-1.4) =$ **$^-3.36$**

17. $(^-\frac{3}{5})(\frac{3}{5}) =$ **$-\frac{9}{25}$**

18. $(^-\frac{4}{5})(2.2) =$ **$^-1.76$**

19. $^-8 \cdot 12 =$ **$^-96$**

20. $(0)(2)(^-213) =$ **0**

Name _____ Date _____

Operations with Real Numbers

Dividing Real Numbers

$$9 \div 4.5 = 2$$

Divide.

1. $\frac{49}{7} =$ **7**

2. $90 \div 15 =$ **6**

3. $(^{-}12) \div (9.9) =$ **$^{-}1.\overline{21}$**

4. $(^{-}\frac{2}{3}) \div (^{-}18) = \frac{1}{27}$

5. $^{-}42 \div 7 =$ **$^{-}6$**

6. $45 \div (^{-}8) =$ **$^{-}5.625$**

7. $^{-}36 \div (4) =$ **$^{-}9$**

8. $(^{-}\frac{3}{5}) \div (\frac{3}{5}) =$ **$^{-}1$**

9. $^{-}72 \div (9) =$ **$^{-}8$**

10. $^{-}21 \div (^{-}9) =$ **$2.\overline{3}$**

11. $\frac{102}{17} =$ **6**

12. $0 \div (^{-}8) =$ **0**

13. $\frac{95}{5} =$ **19**

14. $\frac{63}{^{-}9} =$ **$^{-}7$**

15. $(^{-}3.4) \div (^{-}9.99) =$ **$0.\overline{340}$**

16. $(^{-}56) \div (8.0) =$ **$^{-}7$**

17. $(^{-}\frac{4}{6}) \div (36) =$ **$^{-}\frac{1}{54}$**

18. $32 \div (^{-}8) =$ **$^{-}4$**

19. $(^{-}\frac{4}{5}) \div (^{-}1.6) =$ **0.5**

20. $520 \div (10) =$ **52**

12   CD-104316 • © Carson-Dellosa

Name _____ Date _____

Operations with Real Numbers

Order of Operations

When solving an equation, be sure to follow the **order of operations**.

1. Parentheses
2. Exponents
3. Multiplication & Division
4. Addition & Subtraction

$$28 \div (6 - 4) + 2^2 = 28 \div (6 - 4) + 4 = 28 \div 2 + 4 = 14 + 4 = 18$$

Solve.

1. $3 \times 15 \div 5 =$ **9**

2. $35 \div 5 - 9 =$ **$^{-}2$**

3. $3 + 2 \times 4 =$ **11**

4. $5 \times 2 \times 8 =$ **80**

5. $6 - 40 \div 8 =$ **1**

6. $5(6 + 2) =$ **40**

7. $12 - 30 \div 6 =$ **7**

8. $32 \div 4 \times 3 =$ **24**

9. $5^2 + 3^2 =$ **34**

10. $8 + 3 \times 2 =$ **14**

11. $4 + 12 \div 2 =$ **10**

12. $9 + 20 \div 5 =$ **13**

13. $15 - 75 \div 5 =$ **0**

14. $9 - 3 + 6 =$ **12**

15. $2 \times 8 \div 4 =$ **4**

16. $3 + 3 - 2 =$ **4**

17. $14 - 54 \div 6 =$ **5**

18. $9 \div 3 \times 8 =$ **24**

CD-104316 • © Carson-Dellosa   13

Name _____ Date _____

Operations with Real Numbers

Order of Operations

When solving an equation, be sure to follow the **order of operations**.

1. Parentheses
2. Exponents
3. Multiplication & Division
4. Addition & Subtraction

$$(3^3 + 6 \times 5) - 2 = (27 + 6 \times 5) - 2 = (27 + 30) - 2 = 55$$

Solve.

1. $(3^2 + 2 \times 3) \div 5 =$ **3**

2. $5^2 - 4^2 + 2 =$ **11**

3. $(4 + 2)^2 =$ **36**

4. $(11 - 8)^3 =$ **27**

5. $2(7 + 2) =$ **18**

6. $(9 - 7)^3 - (4 + 3) =$ **1**

7. $(14 - 6)2 =$ **16**

8. $4 + 3(12 - 9) =$ **13**

9. $5^2 - 2^3 =$ **17**

10. $3 \times 8 - (3 \times 2 + 7) =$ **11**

11. $(5^2 - 3 \times 5) \div 2 =$ **5**

12. $7 + 2^2(5 + 2) =$ **35**

13. $3 + 7^2 =$ **52**

14. $(2^2 + 3)^2 - 4 =$ **45**

15. $6 + 7 \times 3 - 9 \times 2 =$ **9**

16. $(2 \times 3) + (21 \div 7) =$ **9**

17. $7^2 - 2(3 \times 3 + 5) =$ **21**

18. $3 + (6 \times 2) =$ **15**

14   CD-104316 • © Carson-Dellosa

Name _____ Date _____

Operations with Real Numbers

Order of Operations

When solving an equation, be sure to follow the **order of operations**.

1. Parentheses
2. Exponents
3. Multiplication & Division
4. Addition & Subtraction

$$5 + (22 + 2^3) \div (^{-}5 - 1) = 5 + (22 + 8) \div (^{-}5 - 1) = 5 + 30 \div (^{-}6) = 5 + (^{-}5) = 0$$

Solve.

1. $8 - 4 \cdot 5(3 - 2) + 3 =$ **$^{-}9$**

2. $12 \div (2 - 7) + 7 =$ **4.6**

3. $(14 - 9) + 4 =$ **9**

4. $\frac{3^2 - 5 \cdot 7 - 4^2}{(^{-}4 - 7 - 12)} + 8 = 2\frac{4}{5}$

5. $9(3 \div 3) + 4(^{-}5 \cdot 9) \div 3 =$ **$^{-}51$**

6. $3 - (6 \cdot 6) - 3 \cdot 0 =$ **$^{-}33$**

7. $36 \div 9 - 8 + 21 \div 3 =$ **3**

8. $5(3 - 8) \cdot 3 + 8 - 3 =$ **$^{-}70$**

9. $3 \cdot 5 + 9 \cdot 7 =$ **78**

10. $\frac{(5 - 9)^2 + 2}{(7 - 8)^2 \cdot 3^2} =$ **2**

11. $4^2 + 3^2 - 7^2 =$ **$^{-}24$**

12. $\frac{3^2 - 10}{4^2 - 12} =$ **$^{-}\frac{1}{4}$**

13. $8^2 - \frac{26}{(4 + 9)} + 4 =$ **66**

14. $\frac{5 \cdot 7 - (3 + 4)}{^{-}2^2 - 2^2 + 3^2} =$ **28**

15. $\frac{4 + 2 \cdot 3 + 4 - 3}{2^2 \cdot 3^2 - 3} =$ **$\frac{1}{3}$**

16. $\frac{3 + 10 - 19 + 32}{3^2 - 1 + 2^2} = 2\frac{1}{6}$

17. $12 \div [3 + (6 + 3)] =$ **1**

18. $3 \cdot (0 - 7) + 8 \div 2^2 =$ **$^{-}19$**

CD-104316 • © Carson-Dellosa   15

Name _____ Date _____

Operations with Real Numbers

Real-Number Operations with Absolute Value

$-|5 - 11| = -|-6| = -6$ $|-4| + |-3| = 4 + 3 = 7$
The **absolute value** of a number is its distance from zero.
For example: $|5| = 5$ $|-6| = 6$ $|0| = 0$

Simplify.

1. $|-3| =$ **3**
2. $|-14| =$ **14**
3. $9 + |-4| =$ **13**
4. $-5|4| + |5| =$ **-15**
5. $|4| - |7| =$ **-3**
6. $|21| + 9 =$ **30**
7. $23 + |8| =$ **31**
8. $|12| - |-15| =$ **-3**
9. $7 - |-23| + |-7| =$ **-9**
10. $|-6| + |8| =$ **14**
11. $-|-3 + 7| =$ **-4**
12. $-|-5 + 10| =$ **-5**
13. $|-9| + |23| =$ **32**
14. $|-17| - |-17| =$ **0**
15. $|1| - |0| + 6 =$ **7**
16. $|-67| - |-17| =$ **50**
17. $|4| - |-12| - 4 =$ **-12**
18. $|3 - 13| =$ **10**
19. $|23| - |-12| =$ **11**
20. $|9| + |-9| =$ **18**

Name _____ Date _____

Variables and Equations

Substitution

Substitute and simplify. $a = 3, b = -9, c = 5$

1. $b^2 + c^2 =$ **106**
2. $-3b + (a + 2c)^2 =$ **196**
3. $2a^3 - (b + c)^2 =$ **38**
4. $(b + c)^2 =$ **16**
5. $(a + b)^2 =$ **36**
6. $abc =$ **-135**
7. $(c - a)^2 =$ **4**
8. $4a - 6b - 2c =$ **56**
9. $(2c - a)^2 =$ **49**
10. $a^2 + b^3 =$ **-720**

Substitute and simplify. $a = -3, b = -2, c = 5$

11. $5c + b^3 =$ **17**
12. $(a + b + c)^2 =$ **0**
13. $3(a + b)^2 =$ **75**
14. $c^2 - 2ab =$ **13**
15. $a^2 - (2b + c)^3 =$ **8**
16. $2c + 5a - 4b =$ **3**
17. $a^2 + b^2 =$ **13**
18. $2a - 4b =$ **2**
19. $a^2 - b^2 =$ **5**
20. $(a - b)^2 =$ **1**

Name _____ Date _____

Variables and Equations

Substitution

Substitute and simplify. $x = 2, y = 4, z = -3$

1. $2z + 4xy =$ **26**
2. $(2x + y + 3z)^2 =$ **1**
3. $10xyz \div 5 =$ **-48**
4. $5x + 2z =$ **4**
5. $(y + z)^3 =$ **1**
6. $2(6 + z) =$ **6**
7. $3(x + y)^2 =$ **108**
8. $2x + y + z =$ **5**
9. $(x - z) + y =$ **9**
10. $6y + 2xz =$ **12**

Substitute and simplify. $w = -5, x = 4, y = 2, z = -8$

11. $2wz - 3xy =$ **56**
12. $2y(z + x) =$ **-16**
13. $wx + yz =$ **-36**
14. $w^2 - x^2 =$ **9**
15. $5(w + x) + 3(7 + z) =$ **-8**
16. $w + (x + 2y + z)^2 =$ **-5**
17. $(z - w)^3 =$ **-27**
18. $(w + x + y)^3 =$ **1**
19. $(2xy) - 2wz =$ **-64**
20. $3w + 2z - xy + z^3 =$ **-551**

Name _____ Date _____

Variables and Equations

Combining Like Terms

$4x + 5y + (-18x) = -14x + 5y$

Combine like terms.

1. $3yz + 5yz =$ **8yz**
2. $3a + 5 + a =$ **4a + 5**
3. $5x - 5y - 8y + 8x =$ **13x - 3y**
4. $18x + 3x =$ **21x**
5. $5 - (-4k) =$ **5 + 4k**
6. $7c - 12c =$ **-5c**
7. $13ab + (-12ab) =$ **ab**
8. $-12x + (-4x) =$ **-16x**
9. $-10n - (-13n) =$ **3n**
10. $12b + (-34b) =$ **-22b**
11. $4.7x - 5.9x =$ **-1.2x**
12. $4x^2 + (-8y) + (-3xy) + 5x^2 + 2xy =$ **9x² - xy - 8y**
13. $4x + 3y + (-5y) + 3xy + y =$ **4x - y + 3xy**
14. $2x - y + 2x + 3xy =$ **4x + 3xy - y**
15. $5x + 7x =$ **12x**
16. $23x + 8 + 6x + 3y =$ **29x + 3y + 8**
17. $-e + 8e =$ **7e**
18. $2xy + 5x + 6xy + 3xy + (-3x) =$ **2x + 11xy**
19. $7s + 5x - 8s =$ **5x - s**
20. $4xy + 7xy + 6x^2y + 3xy^2 =$ **11xy + 6x²y + 3xy²**

Name _____ Date _____

Variables and Equations

Combining Like Terms

$$5(x + 2) + (3x - 7y) + (2x + 4y) = 5x + 10 + 3x - 7y + 2x + 4y = 10x + 10 - 3y$$

Combine like terms.

1. $^-n + 9n + 3 - 8 - 8n = $ **$^-5$**

2. $3(^-4x + 5y) - 3x(2 + 4y) = $ **$^-18x + 15y - 12xy$**

3. $5 - 4y + x + 9y = $ **$x + 5 + 5y$**

4. $^-2x + 3y - 5x - ^-8y + 9y = $ **$^-7x + 20y$**

5. $6(a - b) - 5(2a + 4b) = $ **$^-4a - 26b$**

6. $7(x + 5y) + 3(x + 5y) + 5(3x + 8y) = $ **$25x + 90y$**

7. $12x + 6x + 9x - 3y + (^-7y) + y = $ **$27x - 9y$**

8. $^-21x + (^-2x) = $ **^-23x**

9. $4(x + 9y) - 2(2x + 4y) = $ **$28y$**

10. $4(x + 5y) + (5x + y) = $ **$9x + 21y$**

11. $6x + ^-2y^2 + 4xy^2 + 3x^2 + 5xy^2 = $ **$3x^2 + 6x - 2y^2 + 9xy^2$**

12. $^-2(c - d) + (c - 3d) - 5(c - d) = $ **$^-6c + 4d$**

13. $3x + (^-3y) - (^-4x) + y = $ **$^-x - 2y$**

14. $^-3(4x + ^-2y) - 2(x + 3y) - 2(2x + 6y) = $ **$^-18x - 12y$**

15. $2b + 3(2b + 8a) - 3(8b + 2a) = $ **$^-16b + 18a$**

16. $3[2(^-y^2 + y) - 3] - 3(2x + y) = $ **$^-6y^2 + 3y - 6x - 9$**

17. $2 \cdot 4x \cdot 3y - 4x \cdot 7y = $ **^-4xy**

18. $5(3a^2 - 2b^2) + 3a(a + 3b^2) = $ **$18a^2 + 9ab^2 - 10b^2$**

19. $3c + 4d + 2c + 5d - 4c = $ **$c + 9d$**

20. $4(x^2 + 3y^2) - y(x^2 + 5y) = $ **$4x^2 - xy^2 + 7y^2$**

20 · CD-104316 • © Carson-Dellosa

Name _____ Date _____

Variables and Equations

Solving One-Step Equations (Addition and Subtraction)

$$12 + x = ^-24$$
$$12 + (^-12) + x = ^-24 + (^-12)$$
$$x = ^-36$$

Solve each equation for the given variable.

1. $^-13 + b = 31$ **$b = 44$**

2. $n + \frac{3}{8} = \frac{5}{8}$ **$n = \frac{1}{4}$**

3. $x - 17 = ^-27$ **$x = ^-10$**

4. $27 = v + (^-5)$ **$v = 32$**

5. $^-4 = x - 3$ **$x = ^-1$**

6. $c - 3 = 4.7$ **$c = 7.7$**

7. $a + 5.7 = 18.9$ **$a = 13.2$**

8. $12 - (^-u) = 17$ **$u = 5$**

9. $^-200 = b + (^-73)$ **$b = ^-127$**

10. $^-13 + x = 18$ **$x = 31$**

11. $^-t + (^-7) = ^-56$ **$t = 49$**

12. $3 + x = 9$ **$x = 6$**

13. $z + 3.5 = 4.7$ **$z = 1.2$**

14. $12 + (^-g) = 10$ **$g = 2$**

15. $y - 12 = 15$ **$y = 27$**

16. $2\frac{1}{3} + r = 4\frac{2}{9}$ **$r = 1\frac{8}{9}$**

17. $x + 2 = 2(3 - 4)$ **$x = ^-4$**

18. $s - 5 = 6 + (^-8)$ **$s = 3$**

19. $^-13 = n + (^-39)$ **$n = 26$**

20. $r = 4.4 + 3.9$ **$r = 8.3$**

CD-104316 • © Carson-Dellosa · 21

Name _____ Date _____

Variables and Equations

Solving One-Step Equations (Multiplication and Division)

$$3x = 15$$
$$\frac{3x}{3} = \frac{15}{3}$$
$$x = 5$$

$$-\frac{3}{4y} = ^-6$$
$$-\frac{4}{3} \cdot -\frac{3}{4y} = ^-6 \cdot -\frac{4}{3}$$
$$y = 8$$

Solve each equation for the given variable.

1. $12.8 = 4b$ **$b = 3.2$**

2. $4b = ^-36$ **$b = ^-9$**

3. $^-13h = 169$ **$h = ^-13$**

4. $-\frac{3}{4} = \frac{n}{16}$ **$n = ^-12$**

5. $10x = ^-100$ **$x = ^-10$**

6. $4c = 288$ **$c = 72$**

7. $7x = ^-63$ **$x = ^-9$**

8. $4y = ^-48$ **$y = ^-12$**

9. $6x = ^-36$ **$x = ^-6$**

10. $\frac{8}{k} = \frac{2}{5}$ **$k = 20$**

11. $^-(^-90) = ^-45z$ **$z = ^-2$**

12. $-\frac{x}{8} = \frac{1}{4}$ **$x = ^-2$**

13. $^-50 = 2x$ **$x = ^-25$**

14. $\frac{2}{n} = \frac{1}{9}$ **$n = 18$**

15. $\frac{4}{x} = \frac{2}{9}$ **$x = 18$**

16. $\frac{x}{6} = \frac{6}{9}$ **$x = 4$**

17. $^-35c = 700$ **$c = ^-20$**

18. $^-4x = ^-20$ **$x = 5$**

19. $-\frac{x}{6} = \frac{2}{3}$ **$x = ^-4$**

20. $1.6c = 80$ **$c = 50$**

22 · CD-104316 • © Carson-Dellosa

Name _____ Date _____

Variables and Equations

Solving Basic Equations

$$4x + 4 = 12$$
$$4x + 4 - 4 = 12 - 4$$
$$4x = 8$$
$$x = 2$$

Solve each equation for the given variable.

1. $7x - 12 = 2$ **$x = 2$**

2. $7a - 4 = 24$ **$a = 4$**

3. $4b - 7 = 37$ **$b = 11$**

4. $3c - 9 = 9$ **$c = 6$**

5. $4.7 = ^-3.4m - 5.5$ **$m = ^-3$**

6. $8 - 9y = 35$ **$y = ^-3$**

7. $8 - 12x = 32$ **$x = ^-2$**

8. $1.3x + 5 = ^-5.4$ **$x = ^-8$**

9. $3(x + 4) + 5 = 35$ **$x = 6$**

10. $0 = 25x + 75$ **$x = ^-3$**

11. $3 - \frac{1}{5}x = ^-7$ **$x = 50$**

12. $5 - \frac{1}{2}x = ^-9$ **$x = 28$**

13. $2x = 6 + (^-18)$ **$x = ^-6$**

14. $7 - \frac{1}{9}k = 32$ **$k = ^-225$**

15. $32 = \frac{4}{6}x - 34$ **$x = 99$**

16. $\frac{3}{12}x + 2 = 11$ **$x = 36$**

17. $\frac{2x}{5} + 3 = 9$ **$x = 15$**

18. $\frac{x}{3} - 8 = ^-12$ **$x = ^-12$**

19. $5(e + 5) = ^-10$ **$e = ^-7$**

20. $8 - \frac{1}{2}y = ^-6$ **$y = 28$**

CD-104316 • © Carson-Dellosa · 23

Name _____ Date _____

Variables and Equations

Solving Basic Equations

$9x + 3 = 30$
$9x + 3 - 3 = 30 - 3$
$9x = 27$
$x = 3$

Solve each equation for the given variable.

1. $5t - 8 = ^-28$ $t = ^-4$

2. $4k + 7 = ^-9$ $k = ^-4$

3. $13x + 7 = ^-32$ $x = ^-3$

4. $2x + 12 = 6$ $x = ^-3$

5. $7.2 + 4x = 19.2$ $x = 3$

6. $2(w - 6) = 8$ $w = 10$

7. $7h + 1 = ^-13$ $h = ^-2$

8. $3(c - 2) = 15$ $c = 7$

9. $6x - 5 = ^-41$ $x = ^-6$

10. $^-3 + 2n = ^-15$ $n = ^-6$

11. $5e + (^-9) = 26$ $e = 7$

12. $\frac{m}{3} - 7 = ^-10$ $m = ^-9$

13. $6x - 2 = 34$ $x = 6$

14. $^-8(r - 2) = 40$ $r = ^-3$

15. $5n - 8 = ^-23$ $n = ^-3$

16. $2 + (\frac{1}{5})x = ^-7$ $x = ^-45$

17. $5 - (\frac{1}{2})g = 12$ $g = ^-14$

18. $3x - 4 = 14$ $x = 6$

19. $^-6 = \frac{3u}{4} + 12$ $u = ^-24$

20. $2(f + 7) - 8 = 22$ $f = 8$

24   CD-104316 • © Carson-Dellosa

Name _____ Date _____

Variables and Equations

Solving Basic Equations

$12x + 3 = 123$
$12x + 3 - 3 = 123 - 3$
$12x = 120$
$x = 10$

Solve each equation for the given variable.

1. $4(x - 6) = 8$ $x = 8$

2. $4 + 3g = ^-14$ $g = ^-6$

3. $14a + 5 - 8a = ^-1$ $a = ^-1$

4. $4e + 6 - 11e = ^-8$ $e = 2$

5. $^-9r + 5 = ^-22$ $r = 3$

6. $2m - 9 - 8m = ^-27$ $m = 3$

7. $b + 9 - 2b = 6$ $b = 3$

8. $4j - 9j + 3 = ^-32$ $j = 7$

9. $5(j - 4) + j = ^-8$ $j = 2$

10. $\frac{m}{4} + 6 = 2$ $m = ^-16$

11. $3d - 5 - 2d = ^-9$ $d = ^-4$

12. $^-5 + 6d + 3 = 34$ $d = 6$

13. $2k + 3(k + 4) = ^-3$ $k = ^-3$

14. $5(m - 3) + 2m = 27$ $m = 6$

15. $^-j + 5j + 2 = ^-14$ $j = ^-4$

16. $7t - 3 + 4t = ^-25$ $t = ^-2$

17. $4(c + 2) = ^-28$ $c = ^-9$

18. $12k - 3(5 + 5) = 54$ $k = 7$

19. $3e + 4e + 1 = 36$ $e = 5$

20. $^-6r + 12 - 8r = ^-2$ $r = 1$

CD-104316 • © Carson-Dellosa   25

Name _____ Date _____

Variables and Equations

Solving Equations with Variables on Both Sides

$6x - 7 = x + 33$
$6x - x - 7 = x - x + 33$
$5x - 7 + 7 = 33 + 7$
$5x = 40$
$x = 8$

Solve each equation for the given variables.

1. $7 - 6a = 6 - 7a$ $a = ^-1$

2. $3c - 12 = 14 + 5c$ $c = ^-13$

3. $3x - 3 = ^-3x + ^-3$ $x = 0$

4. $2x - 7 = 3x + 4$ $x = ^-11$

5. $9a + 5 = 3a - 1$ $a = ^-1$

6. $8(x - 3) + 8 = 5x - 22$ $x = ^-2$

7. $5t + 7 = 4t - 9$ $t = ^-16$

8. $^-10x + 6 = ^-7x + ^-9$ $x = 5$

9. $^-7c + 9 = c + 1$ $c = 1$

10. $2x + 6 = 5x - 9$ $x = 5$

11. $\frac{5}{2}x + 3 = \frac{1}{2}x + 15$ $x = 6$

12. $5 + 3x = 7(x + 3)$ $x = ^-4$

13. $12m - 9 = 4m + 15$ $m = 3$

14. $2(x - 4) + 8 = 3x - 8$ $x = 8$

15. $^-6 - (^-2n) = 3n - 6 + 5$ $n = ^-5$

16. $4(2y - 4) = 5y + 2$ $y = 6$

17. $2(r - 4) = 5[r + (^-7)]$ $r = 9$

18. $6(x - 9) = 4(x - 5)$ $x = 17$

19. $4(t + 5) - 3 = 6t - 13$ $t = 15$

20. $4e - 19 = ^-3(e + 4)$ $e = 1$

26   CD-104316 • © Carson-Dellosa

Name _____ Date _____

Variables and Equations

Problem Solving

The sum of three times a number and 25 is 40. Find the number.
$3x + 25 = 40$
$3x + 25 - 25 = 40 - 25$
$3x = 15$
$x = 5$ The number is 5.

Write an equation for each word problem and solve it.

1. The difference of a number and $^-3$ is 8. Find the number.
   Equation $x - (^-3) = 8$ Solution $x = 5$

2. Twice a number added to 9 is 15. Find the number.
   Equation $2x + 9 = 15$ Solution $x = 3$

3. Twelve subtracted from 3 times a number is 15. Find the number.
   Equation $3x - 12 = 15$ Solution $x = 9$

4. The sum of 4 times a number and 5 is $^-7$. Find the number.
   Equation $4x + 5 = ^-7$ Solution $x = ^-3$

5. The product of a number and 5 is 60. Find the number.
   Equation $5x = 60$ Solution $x = 12$

6. The difference of 5 times a number and 6 is 14. Find the number.
   Equation $5x - 6 = 14$ Solution $x = 4$

7. The sum of a number and $^-6$ is 10. Find the number.
   Equation $x + (^-6) = 10$ Solution $x = 16$

8. The quotient of a number and 4 is $^-12$. Find the number.
   Equation $\frac{x}{4} = ^-12$ Solution $x = ^-48$

CD-104316 • © Carson-Dellosa   27

Variables and Equations
Problem Solving

The sum of four times a number and 14 is 74. Find the number.
$4x + 14 = 74$
$4x + 14 - 14 = 74 - 14$
$4x = 60$
$x = 15$ The number is 15.

Write an equation for each word problem and solve it.

1. Six times the difference of a number and 9 is 54. Find the number.
   Equation __$6(x - 9) = 54$__   Solution __$x = 18$__

2. The sum of 8 times a number and 3 is 59. Find the number.
   Equation __$8x + 3 = 59$__   Solution __$x = 7$__

3. The sum of 5 times a number and ⁻11 is ⁻16. Find the number.
   Equation __$5x + (^-11) = ^-16$__   Solution __$x = ^-1$__

4. Twelve times the sum of a number and ⁻8 is 48. Find the number.
   Equation __$12[x + (^-8)] = 48$__   Solution __$x = 12$__

5. The sum of 5 times a number and 2 is ⁻13. Find the number.
   Equation __$5x + 2 = ^-13$__   Solution __$x = ^-3$__

6. The sum of 7 times a number and 11 is 81. Find the number.
   Equation __$7x + 11 = 81$__   Solution __$x = 10$__

7. Three times the sum of a number and ⁻2 is ⁻15. Find the number.
   Equation __$3[x + (^-2)] = ^-15$__   Solution __$x = ^-3$__

8. Five times the sum of a number and 2 is 35. Find the number.
   Equation __$5(x + 2) = 35$__   Solution __$x = 5$__

28   CD-104316 • © Carson-Dellosa

Variables and Equations
Solving Inequalities with Multiple Operations

$^-10n + 5 \le 55$
$^-10n + 5 - 5 \le 55 - 5$
$^-10n \le 50$
$n \ge ^-5$

Solve each inequality and graph its solution set.

1. $^-4(3t + 2) \le 4$
   $t \ge ^-1$

2. $10 - 5x - 20 \ge ^-20$
   $x \le 2$

3. $^-15 > 4x - 7 - 3x - 4$
   $x < ^-4$

4. $4x - 7 < 9$
   $x < 4$

5. $6x - 3 > 33$
   $x > 6$

6. $3(3c - 4) < 15$
   $c < 3$

7. $5x - 1 > 9$
   $x > 2$

8. $5 > 4x - 11$
   $x < 4$

CD-104316 • © Carson-Dellosa   29

Variables and Equations
Solving Inequalities with Variables on Both Sides

$^-10x > 4x - 42$
$^-10x + 10x > 4x + 10x - 42$
$0 > 14x - 42$
$42 > 14x - 42 + 42$
$42 > 14x$
$x < 3$

Solve each inequality and graph its solution set.

1. $7m + 9 \le 6(m + 3)$
   $m \le 9$

2. $3(2x + 4) \ge 7x + 8$
   $x \le 4$

3. $2(k + 4) \le 3(2k - 4)$
   $k \ge 5$

4. $5x + (^-3) > 2(3 + x)$
   $x > 3$

5. $5c + 2 < 2c + (^-7)$
   $c < ^-3$

6. $5x - 20 > 2x + 1$
   $x > 7$

7. $3(s - 4) \ge 4s - 12$
   $s \le 0$

8. $^-9 - e > 3e + 11$
   $e < ^-5$

30   CD-104316 • © Carson-Dellosa

Variables and Equations
Practice Solving Inequalities

Solve each inequality and graph its solution set.

1. $11 \le 6y - 25$
   $y \ge 6$

2. $14 + 3x > 6x - 7$
   $x < 7$

3. $5x \ge ^-20$
   $x \ge ^-4$

4. $^-13t > 52$
   $t < ^-4$

5. $6x - 4 > 2(x - 6)$
   $x > ^-2$

6. $12d < d + 11$
   $d < 1$

7. $14h \le 112$
   $h \le 8$

8. $4a - 3 \le ^-27$
   $a \le ^-6$

9. $\frac{a}{4} + 3 \le 5$
   $a \le 8$

10. $r + 13 \ge 9$
    $r \ge ^-4$

CD-104316 • © Carson-Dellosa   31

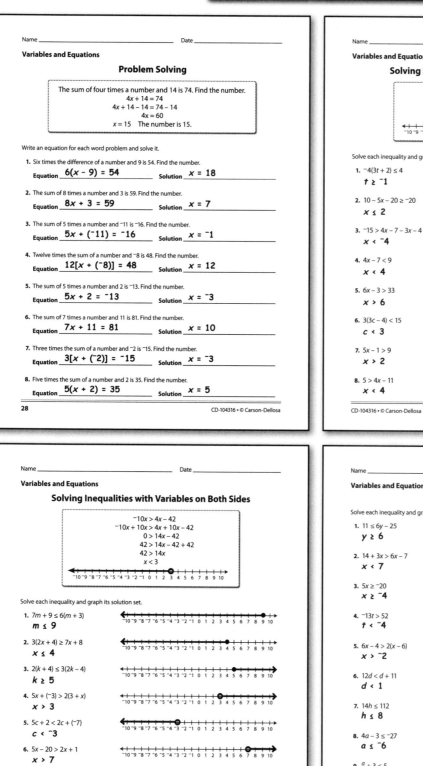

Page 32

Name _____ Date _____

Variables and Equations

Practice Solving Inequalities

Solve each inequality and graph its solution set.

1. $15e - 3 \le 20e + 17$
$e \ge {}^-4$

2. $13x \ge {}^-26$
$x \ge {}^-2$

3. $7c - 8 \ge 6$
$c \ge 2$

4. $5n + 3 \ge {}^-12$
$n \ge {}^-3$

5. $4 + 6r > {}^-8$
$r > {}^-2$

6. $6d < 3d - 18$
$d < {}^-6$

7. ${}^-2a < 10 + 3a$
$a > {}^-2$

8. $4w > 2w + 8$
$w > 4$

9. ${}^-4.2 > 0.6x$
$x < {}^-7$

10. $7k < {}^-35$
$k < {}^-5$

Page 33

Name _____ Date _____

Polynomials

Adding and Subtracting Polynomials

$$(x^2 + 4x + 2) - (2x^2 + 7x - 6) = {}^-x^2 - 3x + 8$$

Add or subtract the polynomials by combining like terms.

1. $(2x^2 + 3x + 2) - (6x^3 - 3x^2 + 8) - ({}^-2x^3 + 9x^2 + 7) =$ ${}^-\mathbf{4x^3 - 4x^2 + 3x - 13}$

2. $(4y^2 - 9y) - ({}^-5y^2 + 8y - 8) =$ $\mathbf{9y^2 - 17y + 8}$

3. $({}^-3x^2 - 4x^3 - 1) - (2x^3 - 7x - 9) - (2x^3 - 2x^2 - 3) =$ ${}^-\mathbf{8x^3 - x^2 + 7x + 11}$

4. $(6x^2 + 2x + 6) - (4x^2 - 2x + 3) + ({}^-5x^2 + 5x + 6) =$ ${}^-\mathbf{3x^2 + 9x + 9}$

5. $({}^-2x^3 + 3x^2 + 9) + ({}^-8x^3 - 2x^2 + {}^-4x) =$ ${}^-\mathbf{10x^3 + x^2 - 4x + 9}$

6. $(2x^2 - 9x - 8) - (2x^3 - 7x^2 + {}^-2) =$ ${}^-\mathbf{2x^3 + 9x^2 - 9x - 6}$

7. $(4x^3 - 2x^2 - 12) + (6x^2 + 3x + 8) =$ $\mathbf{4x^3 + 4x^2 + 3x - 4}$

8. $(3x^4 - 3x + 1) - (4x^3 - 4x - 8) =$ $\mathbf{3x^4 - 4x^3 + x + 9}$

9. $({}^-6x^2 - 3x^3 + 4) + ({}^-7x^3 + 2x + 4) - ({}^-3x^3 + 5x^2 + 2) =$ ${}^-\mathbf{7x^3 - 11x^2 + 2x + 6}$

10. $(4x^2 + 6x + 3) + (3x^2 - 3x - 2) + ({}^-4x^2 + 3x - 9) =$ $\mathbf{3x^2 + 6x - 8}$

11. $(7x^2 - x - 5) - (3x^2 - 3x + 5) =$ $\mathbf{4x^2 + 2x - 10}$

12. $(x^3 - x^2 + 3) - (3x^3 - x^2 + 7) =$ ${}^-\mathbf{2x^3 - 4}$

13. $({}^-2x^2 + 4x - 12) + (5x^2 - 5x) =$ $\mathbf{3x^2 - x - 12}$

14. $(9x^2 - 7x + {}^-4) + (3x^3 - 4x + {}^-5) + ({}^-4x^2 - 2x - 5) =$ $\mathbf{3x^3 + 5x^2 - 13x - 14}$

15. $(4x^3 - 5x^2 - 9) - (6x^3 - 5x - 4) - (5x^3 - 4x^2 - 10) =$ ${}^-\mathbf{7x^3 - x^2 + 5x + 5}$

Page 34

Name _____ Date _____

Polynomials

Raising Exponents to a Power and Multiplying Exponents

Rule: $(x^a)^b = x^{ab}$ Example: $(x^2y^3)^3 = x^6y^9$
Rule: $x^a \cdot x^b = x^{a+b}$ Example: $x^3 \cdot x^5 = x^8$

Multiply the polynomials.

1. $({}^-4xy^3)^3 =$ ${}^-\mathbf{64x^3y^9}$

2. $(x^2y^3)(x^3y) =$ $\mathbf{x^5y^4}$

3. $({}^-6x^4y^6)^3 =$ ${}^-\mathbf{216x^{12}y^{18}}$

4. $(5x^2y^4)^3 =$ $\mathbf{125x^6y^{12}}$

5. $(6x^5y^4)^3 =$ $\mathbf{216x^{15}y^{12}}$

6. $(2x)^4 =$ $\mathbf{16x^4}$

7. $({}^-3x^2y)^3 =$ ${}^-\mathbf{27x^6y^3}$

8. $(x^3y)^2 =$ $\mathbf{x^6y^2}$

9. $({}^-2x^2y)^4 =$ $\mathbf{16x^8y^4}$

10. $(x^2y^3)(x^3y^2) =$ $\mathbf{x^5y^5}$

11. $({}^-4x^3y^3)^4 =$ $\mathbf{256x^{12}y^{12}}$

12. $(3xy^3)({}^-4x^2y^4)^2(xy^3) =$ $\mathbf{48x^6y^{14}}$

13. $({}^-3x^3y)^3 =$ ${}^-\mathbf{27x^9y^3}$

14. $({}^-2x^4y^5)^3 =$ ${}^-\mathbf{8x^{12}y^{15}}$

15. $(3x^2y^3)^4 =$ $\mathbf{81x^8y^{12}}$

16. $(6x^2y^3)^0 =$ $\mathbf{1}$

17. $(x^3y^3)^3 =$ $\mathbf{x^9y^9}$

18. $(5xy^2)({}^-5xy^2) =$ ${}^-\mathbf{25x^2y^5}$

19. $({}^-3x^2y^3)^2 =$ $\mathbf{9x^4y^6}$

20. $(8xy)^2 =$ $\mathbf{64x^2y^2}$

Page 35

Name _____ Date _____

Polynomials

Multiplying Exponents

Rule: $x^a \cdot x^b = x^{a+b}$ Example: $a^4 \cdot a^3 = a^7$

Multiply the polynomials.

1. $c \cdot c^2 \cdot c^3 =$ $\mathbf{c^6}$

2. $e \cdot e^2 \cdot e^3 \cdot e^4 \cdot e^5 =$ $\mathbf{e^{15}}$

3. $a^3 \cdot a^4 \cdot a^7 \cdot a =$ $\mathbf{a^{15}}$

4. $(3xy^2)(2x^2y^3) =$ $\mathbf{6x^3y^5}$

5. $(2a^2b)(4ab^2) =$ $\mathbf{8a^3b^3}$

6. $(5f)({}^-3f^3)(2f) =$ ${}^-\mathbf{30f^5}$

7. $(m^2n)(4mn^2)(mn) =$ $\mathbf{4m^4n^4}$

8. $(4k^2)({}^-3k)(3k^5) =$ ${}^-\mathbf{36k^8}$

9. $({}^-2c^4)(4cd)({}^-cd^2) =$ $\mathbf{8c^6d^3}$

10. $(3x^3)(3x^4)({}^-3x^2) =$ ${}^-\mathbf{27x^9}$

11. $({}^-1)(x)({}^-x^2)(x^3)({}^-x^2) =$ ${}^-\mathbf{x^8}$

12. $(3x^2)({}^-3x^5) =$ ${}^-\mathbf{9x^7}$

13. $(c^2h)(3ch^3)(2c^3h^4) =$ $\mathbf{6c^6h^8}$

14. $({}^-4p^3)({}^-4p^6)({}^-2p^9) =$ ${}^-\mathbf{32p^{18}}$

15. $(12c^3)(2g^3)(4ch) =$ $\mathbf{96c^4g^3h}$

16. $(4x^2y^3)(x^3y)({}^-x^2y^2) =$ ${}^-\mathbf{4x^7y^6}$

17. $({}^-4f^3)({}^-3m^3) =$ $\mathbf{12f^3m^3}$

18. $(2c^2d^2)({}^-5cd^4) =$ ${}^-\mathbf{10c^3d^6}$

19. $(4c^2)({}^-5c^7) =$ ${}^-\mathbf{20c^9}$

20. $(3x)({}^-4y^2)(6x^3y) =$ ${}^-\mathbf{72x^4y^3}$

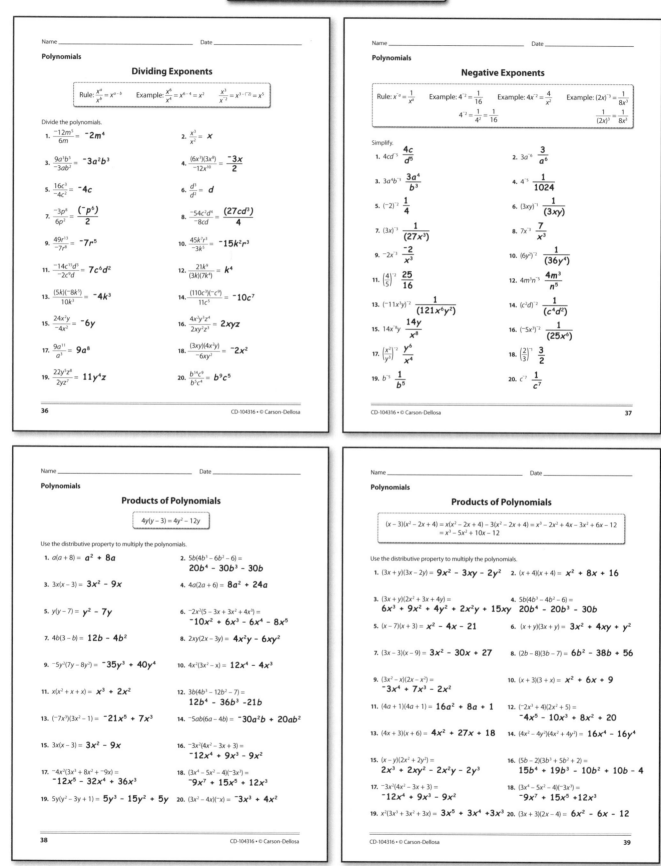

Name _____ Date _____

Polynomials

Dividing Exponents

> Rule: $\dfrac{x^a}{x^b} = x^{a-b}$ Example: $\dfrac{x^6}{x^4} = x^{6-4} = x^2$ $\dfrac{x^3}{x^{-2}} = x^{3-(-2)} = x^5$

Divide the polynomials.

1. $\dfrac{-12m^5}{6m} = $ **$-2m^4$**

2. $\dfrac{x^3}{x^2} = $ **x**

3. $\dfrac{9a^3b^5}{-3ab^2} = $ **$-3a^2b^3$**

4. $\dfrac{(6x^3)(3x^8)}{-12x^{10}} = $ **$\dfrac{-3x}{2}$**

5. $\dfrac{16c^3}{-4c^2} = $ **$-4c$**

6. $\dfrac{d^3}{d^2} = $ **d**

7. $\dfrac{-3p^8}{6p^2} = $ **$\dfrac{(-p^6)}{2}$**

8. $\dfrac{-54c^2d^4}{-8cd} = $ **$\dfrac{(27cd^3)}{4}$**

9. $\dfrac{49r^{13}}{-7r^8} = $ **$-7r^5$**

10. $\dfrac{45k^7r^3}{-3k^5} = $ **$-15k^2r^3$**

11. $\dfrac{-14c^{15}d^3}{-2c^9d} = $ **$7c^6d^2$**

12. $\dfrac{21k^9}{(3k)(7k^4)} = $ **k^4**

13. $\dfrac{(5k)(-8k^5)}{10k^3} = $ **$-4k^3$**

14. $\dfrac{(110c^3)(-c^9)}{11c^5} = $ **$-10c^7$**

15. $\dfrac{24x^2y}{-4x^2} = $ **$-6y$**

16. $\dfrac{4x^3y^3z^4}{2xy^2z^3} = $ **$2xyz$**

17. $\dfrac{9a^{11}}{a^3} = $ **$9a^8$**

18. $\dfrac{(3xy)(4x^2y)}{-6xy^2} = $ **$-2x^2$**

19. $\dfrac{22y^5z^8}{2yz^7} = $ **$11y^4z$**

20. $\dfrac{b^{14}c^9}{b^5c^4} = $ **b^9c^5**

36   CD-104316 • © Carson-Dellosa

Name _____ Date _____

Polynomials

Negative Exponents

> Rule: $x^{-a} = \dfrac{1}{x^a}$ Example: $4^{-2} = \dfrac{1}{16}$ Example: $4x^{-2} = \dfrac{4}{x^2}$ Example: $(2x)^{-3} = \dfrac{1}{8x^3}$
> $4^{-2} = \dfrac{1}{4^2} = \dfrac{1}{16}$ $\dfrac{1}{(2x)^3} = \dfrac{1}{8x^3}$

Simplify.

1. $4cd^{-5}$ **$\dfrac{4c}{d^5}$**

2. $3a^{-6}$ **$\dfrac{3}{a^6}$**

3. $3a^4b^{-3}$ **$\dfrac{3a^4}{b^3}$**

4. 4^{-5} **$\dfrac{1}{1024}$**

5. $(-2)^{-2}$ **$\dfrac{1}{4}$**

6. $(3xy)^{-1}$ **$\dfrac{1}{(3xy)}$**

7. $(3x)^{-3}$ **$\dfrac{1}{(27x^3)}$**

8. $7x^{-3}$ **$\dfrac{7}{x^3}$**

9. $-2x^{-3}$ **$\dfrac{-2}{x^3}$**

10. $(6y^2)^{-2}$ **$\dfrac{1}{(36y^4)}$**

11. $\left(\dfrac{4}{5}\right)^{-2}$ **$\dfrac{25}{16}$**

12. $4m^3n^{-5}$ **$\dfrac{4m^3}{n^5}$**

13. $(-11xy)^{-2}$ **$\dfrac{1}{(121x^6y^2)}$**

14. $(c^2d)^{-2}$ **$\dfrac{1}{(c^4d^2)}$**

15. $14x^{-8}y$ **$\dfrac{14y}{x^8}$**

16. $(-5x^3)^{-2}$ **$\dfrac{1}{(25x^6)}$**

17. $\left(\dfrac{x^2}{y^3}\right)^{-2}$ **$\dfrac{y^6}{x^4}$**

18. $\left(\dfrac{2}{3}\right)^{-1}$ **$\dfrac{3}{2}$**

19. b^{-5} **$\dfrac{1}{b^5}$**

20. c^{-7} **$\dfrac{1}{c^7}$**

CD-104316 • © Carson-Dellosa   37

Name _____ Date _____

Polynomials

Products of Polynomials

> $4y(y-3) = 4y^2 - 12y$

Use the distributive property to multiply the polynomials.

1. $a(a+8) = $ **$a^2 + 8a$**

2. $5b(4b^3 - 6b^2 - 6) = $ **$20b^4 - 30b^3 - 30b$**

3. $3x(x-3) = $ **$3x^2 - 9x$**

4. $4a(2a+6) = $ **$8a^2 + 24a$**

5. $y(y-7) = $ **$y^2 - 7y$**

6. $-2x^2(5 - 3x + 3x^2 + 4x^3) = $ **$-10x^2 + 6x^3 - 6x^4 - 8x^5$**

7. $4b(3-b) = $ **$12b - 4b^2$**

8. $2xy(2x - 3y) = $ **$4x^2y - 6xy^2$**

9. $-5y^2(7y - 8y^2) = $ **$-35y^3 + 40y^4$**

10. $4x^2(3x^2 - x) = $ **$12x^4 - 4x^3$**

11. $x(x^2 + x + x) = $ **$x^3 + 2x^2$**

12. $3b(4b^3 - 12b^2 - 7) = $ **$12b^4 - 36b^3 - 21b$**

13. $(-7x^3)(3x^2 - 1) = $ **$-21x^5 + 7x^3$**

14. $-5ab(6a - 4b) = $ **$-30a^2b + 20ab^2$**

15. $3x(x-3) = $ **$3x^2 - 9x$**

16. $-3x^2(4x^2 - 3x + 3) = $ **$-12x^4 + 9x^3 - 9x^2$**

17. $-4x^2(3x^3 + 8x^2 + -9x) = $ **$-12x^5 - 32x^4 + 36x^3$**

18. $(3x^4 - 5x^2 - 4)(-3x^3) = $ **$-9x^7 + 15x^5 + 12x^3$**

19. $5y(y^2 - 3y + 1) = $ **$5y^3 - 15y^2 + 5y$**

20. $(3x^2 - 4x)(-x) = $ **$-3x^3 + 4x^2$**

38   CD-104316 • © Carson-Dellosa

Name _____ Date _____

Polynomials

Products of Polynomials

> $(x-3)(x^2 - 2x + 4) = x(x^2 - 2x + 4) - 3(x^2 - 2x + 4) = x^3 - 2x^2 + 4x - 3x^2 + 6x - 12$
> $= x^3 - 5x^2 + 10x - 12$

Use the distributive property to multiply the polynomials.

1. $(3x+y)(3x-2y) = $ **$9x^2 - 3xy - 2y^2$**

2. $(x+4)(x+4) = $ **$x^2 + 8x + 16$**

3. $(3x+y)(2x^2 + 3x + 4y) = $ **$6x^3 + 9x^2 + 4y^2 + 2x^2y + 15xy$**

4. $5b(4b^3 - 4b^2 - 6) = $ **$20b^4 - 20b^3 - 30b$**

5. $(x-7)(x+3) = $ **$x^2 - 4x - 21$**

6. $(x+y)(3x+y) = $ **$3x^2 + 4xy + y^2$**

7. $(3x-3)(x-9) = $ **$3x^2 - 30x + 27$**

8. $(2b-8)(3b-7) = $ **$6b^2 - 38b + 56$**

9. $(3x^2 - x)(2x - x^2) = $ **$-3x^4 + 7x^3 - 2x^2$**

10. $(x+3)(3+x) = $ **$x^2 + 6x + 9$**

11. $(4a+1)(4a+1) = $ **$16a^2 + 8a + 1$**

12. $(-2x^3 + 4)(2x^2 + 5) = $ **$-4x^5 - 10x^3 + 8x^2 + 20$**

13. $(4x+3)(x+6) = $ **$4x^2 + 27x + 18$**

14. $(4x^2 - 4y^2)(4x^2 + 4y^2) = $ **$16x^4 - 16y^4$**

15. $(x-y)(2x^2 + 2y^2) = $ **$2x^3 + 2xy^2 - 2x^2y - 2y^3$**

16. $(5b-2)(3b^3 + 5b^2 + 2) = $ **$15b^4 + 19b^3 - 10b^2 + 10b - 4$**

17. $-3x^2(4x^2 - 3x + 3) = $ **$-12x^4 + 9x^3 - 9x^2$**

18. $(3x^4 - 5x^2 - 4)(-3x^3) = $ **$-9x^7 + 15x^5 + 12x^3$**

19. $x^2(3x^3 + 3x^2 + 3x) = $ **$3x^5 + 3x^4 + 3x^3$**

20. $(3x+3)(2x-4) = $ **$6x^2 - 6x - 12$**

CD-104316 • © Carson-Dellosa   39

Name _____ Date _____

Polynomials

Multiplying Binomials

> Rule: $(a + b)(a - b) = a^2 - b^2$
> Example: $(x - 3)(x + 3) = x^2 + 3x - 3x - 9 = x^2 - 9$

Use the FOIL method or DOTS rule to multiply the binomials.

1. $(2x + y)(2x - y) = $ **$4x^2 - y^2$**
2. $(b - 5)(b + 5) = $ **$b^2 - 25$**
3. $(x - y)(2x + 2y) = $ **$2x^2 - 2y^2$**
4. $(4b^2 - 4)(4b^2 + 4) = $ **$16b^4 - 16$**
5. $(7x - 3y)(7x + 3y) = $ **$49x^2 - 9y^2$**
6. $(x + 6)(x - 6) = $ **$x^2 - 36$**
7. $(7x + y)(7x - y) = $ **$49x^2 - y^2$**
8. $(^-5x^2 + 3)(^-5x^2 - 3) = $ **$25x^4 - 9$**
9. $(3a - b)(3a + b) = $ **$9a^2 - b^2$**
10. $(x + 2)(x - 2) = $ **$x^2 - 4$**
11. $(12b - 5)(12b + 5) = $ **$144b^2 - 25$**
12. $(x - yz)(x + yz) = $ **$x^2 - y^2z^2$**
13. $(8x^2 - 12)(8x^2 + 12) = $ **$64x^4 - 144$**
14. $(3x + 13)(3x - 2) = $ **$9x^2 + 33x - 26$**
15. $(c + 2d)(c - 2d) = $ **$c^2 - 4d^2$**
16. $(3b + 6)(3b - 6) = $ **$9b^2 - 36$**
17. $(x^2 - 8x)(x^2 + 8x) = $ **$x^4 - 64x^2$**
18. $(2x^2 - y^2)(2x^2 + y^2) = $ **$4x^4 - y^4$**
19. $(12 + b)(12 - b) = $ **$144 - b^2$**
20. $(3x^2 - x)(3x^2 + x) = $ **$9x^4 - x^2$**

Name _____ Date _____

Polynomials

Squaring Binomials

> Rules: $(a + b)^2 = a^2 + 2ab + b^2$
> $(a - b)^2 = a^2 - 2ab + b^2$

Use the FOIL method or Squares of Binomial Formula to multiply the binomials.

1. $(x - 4y)^2 = $ **$x^2 - 8xy + 16y^2$**
2. $(3b - 3c)^2 = $ **$9b^2 - 18bc + 9c^2$**
3. $(x - 2y)^2 = $ **$x^2 - 4xy + 4y^2$**
4. $(2x - 6y)^2 = $ **$4x^2 - 24xy + 36y^2$**
5. $(7b^2 - 3c)^2 = $ **$49b^4 - 42b^2c + 9c^2$**
6. $(4c + 9d)^2 = $ **$16c^2 + 72cd + 81d^2$**
7. $(5x^2 - 5y)^2 = $ **$25x^4 - 50x^2y + 25y^2$**
8. $(2x - 3y)^2 = $ **$4x^2 - 12xy + 9y^2$**
9. $(^-4x + 3y)^2 = $ **$16x^2 - 24xy + 9y^2$**
10. $(4m^2 - 2n)^2 = $ **$16m^4 - 16m^2n + 4n^2$**
11. $(x^2 - 7y)^2 = $ **$x^4 - 14x^2y + 49y^2$**
12. $(4x^2 - 4y^2)^2 = $ **$16x^4 - 32x^2y^2 + 16y^4$**
13. $(7x - 5y)^2 = $ **$49x^2 - 70xy + 25y^2$**
14. $(2b^2 - 2c^2)^2 = $ **$4b^4 - 8b^2c^2 + 4c^4$**
15. $(4a + b)^2 = $ **$16a^2 + 8ab + b^2$**
16. $(2b + 5a)^2 = $ **$4b^2 + 20ab + 25a^2$**
17. $(2x + 3v)^2 = $ **$4x^2 + 12xv + 9v^2$**
18. $(5x + 7)^2 = $ **$25x^2 + 70x + 49$**
19. $(3a - 7b)^2 = $ **$9a^2 - 42ab + 49b^2$**
20. $(^-6x + 3y)^2 = $ **$36x^2 - 36xy + 9y^2$**

Name _____ Date _____

Polynomials

Area and Perimeter

Find the perimeter of each polygon.

1. Triangle sides $4y^3$, $4y^3$, base $4y^3 - 4$
$P = $ **$12y^3 - 4$**

2. Rectangle $x^2 + 3x - 1$, $x^2 - 3$
$P = $ **$4x^2 + 6x - 8$**

3. Triangle sides $5y^2$, $5y^2$, base $6y^2 - 4$
$P = $ **$16y^2 - 4$**

4. Rectangle $5x^2 + 2$, $4x^2$
$P = $ **$18x^2 + 4$**

Find the area of each polygon.

> **Triangle** Area: $A = \frac{1}{2}bh$
> **Rectangle** Area: $A = lw$
> **Square** Area: $A = s^2$

5. Triangle legs $6x$, $8x + 3$
$A = $ **$24x^2 + 9x$**

6. Rectangle $x^2 + 3x - 1$, $3x$
$A = $ **$(3x^3 + 9x^2 - 3x)$**

7. Square $5x$
$A = $ **$(25x^2)$**

Name _____ Date _____

Factoring

Factoring Monomials from Polynomials

> To factor a polynomial, write the polynomial as a product of other polynomials.
> For example, $3x^2 - 6x$ can be written as $3x(x - 2)$.
> $3x$ is the Greatest Common Factor (GCF) of $3x^2$ and $6x$.
> $3x$ is a Common Monomial Factor of the terms of the binomial.
> $x - 2$ is a Binomial Factor of $3x^2 - 6$.

Factor.

1. $3x^2 - 12x^3 = $ **$3x^2(1 - 4x)$**
2. $2x^3 - x^4 = $ **$x^3(2 - x)$**
3. $3a^5 - a^3 = $ **$a^3(3a^2 - 1)$**
4. $x^5 + 2x^2 = $ **$x^2(x^3 + 2)$**
5. $24b^2 + 16b = $ **$8b(3b + 2)$**
6. $5x^3 - 7x^2 = $ **$x^2(5x - 7)$**
7. $2x^3 + 6x^2 = $ **$2x^2(x + 3)$**
8. $x^3 - 5x^2 = $ **$x^2(x - 5)$**
9. $15c - 3c^2 = $ **$3c(5 - c)$**
10. $5x^5 - 12x^2 = $ **$x^2(5x^3 - 12)$**
11. $3x^5 + 4x^4 - 4x^2 = $ **$x^2(3x^3 + 4x^2 - 4)$**
12. $9a^2 - 18a = $ **$9a(a - 2)$**
13. $14b^3 - 7b^2 = $ **$7b^2(2b - 1)$**
14. $x^2 + x = $ **$x(x + 1)$**
15. $16a^5b^3 + 32a^4b = $ **$16a^4b(ab^2 + 2)$**
16. $x^3y^4 + x^2y^2 = $ **$x^2y^2(xy^2 + 1)$**
17. $x^2 + x^4 + x^3 = $ **$x^2(1 + x^2 + x)$**
18. $x^5 + 3x^2 = $ **$x^2(x^3 + 3)$**
19. $x^2 + 3x^4 + 6x = $ **$x(x + 3x^3 + 6)$**
20. $7x^2 - 21x^3 - 14x^4 = $ **$7x^2(1 - 3x - 2x^2)$**

Name _____ Date _____

Factoring

Factoring Trinomials of the Form $x^2 + bx + c$

$$a^2 - 9a + 14 = (a - 7)(a - 2)$$

Factor.

1. $t^2 + 13t + 42 =$ $(t + 7)(t + 6)$ 2. $x^2 + x - 90 =$ $(x + 10)(x - 9)$

3. $c^2 + c - 30 =$ $(c + 6)(c - 5)$ 4. $x^2 + 15xy + 44y^2 =$
$(x + 4y)(x + 11y)$

5. $y^2 - 13y + 42 =$ $(y - 6)(y - 7)$ 6. $x^2 - x - 6 =$ $(x - 3)(x + 2)$

7. $x^2 - 13x + 12 =$ $(x - 12)(x - 1)$ 8. $x^2 - 13x + 30 =$ $(x - 10)(x - 3)$

9. $x^2 - 9x + 18 =$ $(x - 3)(x - 6)$ 10. $x^2 - 8x + 16 =$ $(x - 4)(x - 4)$

11. $x^2 - 12xy + 32y^2 =$ $(x - 8y)(x - 4y)$ 12. $x^2 + 14x + 49 =$ $(x + 7)(x + 7)$

13. $a^2 - 10ab - 24b^2 =$ $(a - 12b)(a + 2b)$ 14. $m^2 - 3mn + 2n^2 =$ $(m - 2n)(m - n)$

15. $n^2 + 6n - 16 =$ $(n + 8)(n - 2)$ 16. $b^2 - 4b - 45 =$ $(b - 9)(b + 5)$

17. $x^2 + 12x + 35 =$ $(x + 7)(x + 5)$ 18. $y^2 - 12y + 36 =$ $(y - 6)(y - 6)$

19. $c^2 - 10c + 21 =$ $(c - 7)(c - 3)$ 20. $x^2 + 6x - 40 =$ $(x + 10)(x - 4)$

CD-104316 • © Carson-Dellosa

Name _____ Date _____

Factoring

Factoring Trinomials of the Form $x^2 + bx + c$

$$x^2 + 2x - 15 = (x + 5)(x - 3)$$

Factor.

1. $x^2 + 4x + 4 =$ $(x + 2)(x + 2)$ 2. $x^2 - 7x + 6 =$ $(x - 6)(x - 1)$

3. $x^2 + 7x + 12 =$ $(x + 3)(x + 4)$ 4. $x^2 + 13x + 22 =$ $(x + 11)(x + 2)$

5. $x^2 - 8x + 15 =$ $(x - 3)(x - 5)$ 6. $x^2 + 8xy - 33y^2 =$
$(x + 11y)(x - 3y)$

7. $x^2 - 15x + 56 =$ $(x - 7)(x - 8)$ 8. $x^2 + 14x + 40 =$ $(x + 10)(x + 4)$

9. $x^2 + 18x + 45 =$ $(x + 15)(x + 3)$ 10. $x^2 + 2x - 35 =$ $(x + 7)(x - 5)$

11. $x^2 + 4x - 32 =$ $(x + 8)(x - 4)$ 12. $x^2 - 6x - 16 =$ $(x - 8)(x + 2)$

13. $x^2 + 2xy - 63y^2 =$ $(x + 9y)(x - 7y)$ 14. $x^2 + 23x + 132 =$ $(x + 11)(x + 12)$

15. $x^2 - 14x - 72 =$ $(x + 4)(x - 18)$ 16. $x^2 + 5xy + 6y^2 =$ $(x + 2y)(x + 3y)$

17. $x^2 - xy - 2y^2 =$ $(x - 2y)(x + y)$ 18. $x^2 - 14xy + 24y^2 =$
$(x - 12y)(x - 2y)$

19. $x^2 + 16x + 28 =$ $(x + 14)(x + 2)$ 20. $x^2 - 16x + 39 =$ $(x - 3)(x - 13)$

CD-104316 • © Carson-Dellosa

Name _____ Date _____

Factoring

Factoring Trinomials of the Form $ax^2 + bx + c$

$$2x^2 - 8x - 10 = 2(x^2 - 4x - 5) = 2(x - 5)(x + 1)$$

Factor.

1. $12x^2 - 156x + 144 =$ $12(x - 12)(x - 1)$ 2. $6x^2 - 15x + 6 =$ $3(2x - 1)(x - 2)$

3. $2x^2 + 9x + 10 =$ $(2x + 5)(x + 2)$ 4. $4x^2 - 18x + 20 =$ $2(2x - 5)(x - 2)$

5. $3x^2 - 10x + 7 =$ $(3x - 7)(x - 1)$ 6. $3x^2 - 5x - 12 =$ $(3x + 4)(x - 3)$

7. $3x^2 - 4x - 32 =$ $(3x + 8)(x - 4)$ 8. $5x^2 + 25x + 30 =$ $5(x + 3)(x + 2)$

9. $3x^2 - 20x - 7 =$ $(3x + 1)(x - 7)$ 10. $6x^2 - 15x - 21 =$ $3(2x - 7)(x + 1)$

11. $7c^2 - 16c + 9 =$ $(7c - 9)(c - 1)$ 12. $7x^2 - 26x - 8 =$ $(7x + 2)(x - 4)$

13. $2x^2 + 17x + 21 =$ $(2x + 3)(x + 7)$ 14. $6a^2 - 21a + 15 =$ $3(2a - 5)(a - 1)$

15. $2y^2 - 17y + 35 =$ $(2y - 7)(y - 5)$ 16. $12x^2 - 6x - 18 =$ $6(2x - 3)(x + 1)$

17. $4x^2 + 7x - 15 =$ $(4x - 5)(x + 3)$ 18. $6x^2 - 25x - 25 =$ $(6x + 5)(x - 5)$

19. $4x^2 - 23x + 15 =$ $(4x - 3)(x - 5)$ 20. $3x^2 + 19x + 20 =$ $(3x + 4)(x + 5)$

CD-104316 • © Carson-Dellosa

Name _____ Date _____

Factoring

Factoring Trinomials of the Form $ax^2 + bx + c$

$$2x^2 - 5x - 12 = (2x + 3)(x - 4)$$

Factor.

1. $6x^2 - 14x - 12 =$ $2(x - 3)(3x + 2)$ 2. $2x^2 + 13x + 6 =$ $(2x + 1)(x + 6)$

3. $4x^2 - 15x + 9 =$ $(4x - 3)(x - 3)$ 4. $6x^2 - 21x - 12 =$ $3(2x + 1)(x - 4)$

5. $6x^2 - 5x - 6 =$ $(3x + 2)(2x - 3)$ 6. $9x^2 - 9x - 28 =$ $(3x + 4)(3x - 7)$

7. $5x^2 - 24x + 16 =$ $(5x - 4)(x - 4)$ 8. $15x^2 + 11x - 14 =$ $(5x + 7)(3x - 2)$

9. $4x^2 + 4x - 15 =$ $(2x - 3)(2x + 5)$ 10. $10x^2 - 28x - 6 =$ $2(x - 3)(5x + 1)$

11. $14x^2 - 16x + 2 =$ $2(7x - 1)(x - 1)$ 12. $7x^2 + 17x + 6 =$ $(7x + 3)(x + 2)$

13. $12x^2 - 35x + 25 =$ $(4x - 5)(3x - 5)$ 14. $2x^2 - 2x - 40 =$ $2(x - 5)(x + 4)$

15. $4x^2 - 7x - 15 =$ $(4x + 5)(x - 3)$ 16. $11x^2 - 122x + 11 =$ $(11x - 1)(x - 11)$

17. $2x^2 + 17x + 35 =$ $(2x + 7)(x + 5)$ 18. $2x^2 + 7x + 3 =$ $(2x + 1)(x + 3)$

19. $4x^2 - x - 5 =$ $(4x - 5)(x + 1)$ 20. $12x^2 + 9x - 3 =$ $3(4x - 1)(x + 1)$

CD-104316 • © Carson-Dellosa

Page 48 (top left)

Name _____ Date _____

Factoring

Factoring Trinomials That Are Quadratic in Form

$$x^4 - x^2 - 12 = (x^2)^2 - (x^2) - 12 = (x^2 - 4)(x^2 + 3)$$

Factor.

1. $x^2y^2 + 10xy + 24 =$ **$(xy + 4)(xy + 6)$**
2. $x^4y^4 - x^2y^2 - 12 =$ **$(x^2y^2 + 3)(x^2y^2 - 4)$**
3. $2x^2 - 5x - 12 =$ **$(2x + 3)(x - 4)$**
4. $2x^4 + 16x^2 + 30 =$ **$(2x^2 + 10)(x^2 + 3)$**
5. $x^4 - 8x^2 + 15 =$ **$(x^2 - 3)(x^2 - 5)$**
6. $7x^4 - 11x^2 - 6 =$ **$(7x^2 + 3)(x^2 - 2)$**
7. $2x^4 - 7x^2 - 15 =$ **$(2x^2 + 3)(x^2 - 5)$**
8. $y^4 + 6y^2 - 16 =$ **$(y^2 - 2)(y^2 + 8)$**
9. $8x^4 - 23x^2 - 3 =$ **$(8x^2 + 1)(x^2 - 3)$**
10. $6a^6 - 5a^3b^3 - 25b^6 =$ **$(3a^3 + 5b^3)(2a^3 - 5b^3)$**
11. $3x^4 + 20x^2 + 33 =$ **$(3x^2 + 11)(x^2 + 3)$**
12. $4x^4y^4 - 2x^2y^2 - 56 =$ **$(2x^2y^2 + 7)(2x^2y^2 - 8)$**
13. $6x^2y^2 - 29xy + 23 =$ **$(6xy - 23)(xy - 1)$**
14. $x^4y^4 - 19x^2y^2 + 34 =$ **$(x^2y^2 - 2)(x^2y^2 - 17)$**
15. $y^4 - y^2 - 12 =$ **$(y^2 + 3)(y^2 - 4)$**
16. $x^2y^2 - 18xy + 32 =$ **$(xy - 2)(xy - 16)$**
17. $2x^4y^4 - 17x^2y^2 - 30 =$ **$(2x^2y^2 + 3)(x^2y^2 - 10)$**
18. $2x^2 - 13x + 15 =$ **$(2x - 3)(x - 5)$**
19. $x^2y^2 - 8xy + 15 =$ **$(xy - 3)(xy - 5)$**
20. $x^4y^4 - 8x^2y^2 + 12 =$ **$(x^2y^2 - 6)(x^2y^2 - 2)$**

Page 49 (top right)

Name _____ Date _____

Factoring

Factoring Difference of Two Squares

Rule: $a^2 - b^2 = (a + b)(a - b)$ Example: $x^2 - 49 = (x + 7)(x - 7)$

Factor.

1. $a^2 - 4 =$ **$(a - 2)(a + 2)$**
2. $b^2 - 9 =$ **$(b - 3)(b + 3)$**
3. $1 - 9x^2 =$ **$(1 - 3x)(1 + 3x)$**
4. $x^2 - 25 =$ **$(x - 5)(x + 5)$**
5. $x^2y^2 - 36 =$ **$(xy - 6)(xy + 6)$**
6. $x^2 - 100 =$ **$(x + 10)(x - 10)$**
7. $y^2 - 81 =$ **$(y - 9)(y + 9)$**
8. $c^2 - 16 =$ **$(c - 4)(c + 4)$**
9. $a^2 - 49 =$ **$(a - 7)(a + 7)$**
10. $49x^2 - 16y^4 =$ **$(7x - 4y^2)(7x + 4y^2)$**
11. $16x^2 - 121 =$ **$(4x - 11)(4x + 11)$**
12. $25 - x^2y^2 =$ **$(5 - xy)(5 + xy)$**
13. $64 - x^4y^4 =$ **$(8 - x^2y^2)(8 + x^2y^2)$**
14. $y^2 - 64 =$ **$(y - 8)(y + 8)$**
15. $81x^2 - 4 =$ **$(9x - 2)(9x + 2)$**
16. $16 - 81x^2 =$ **$(4 - 9x)(4 + 9x)$**
17. $x^2y^2 - 121 =$ **$(xy - 11)(xy + 11)$**
18. $49x^2 - 36 =$ **$(7x - 6)(7x + 6)$**
19. $4x^2 - y^2 =$ **$(2x - y)(2x + y)$**
20. $4x^2 - 1 =$ **$(2x - 1)(2x + 1)$**

Page 50 (bottom left)

Name _____ Date _____

Factoring

Factoring Perfect Square Trinomials

Rules: $a^2 + 2ab + b^2 = (a + b)^2$ $a^2 - 2ab + b^2 = (a - b)^2$
Examples: $9x^2 + 6x + 1 = (3x + 1)^2$ $x^2 - 6x + 9 = (x - 3)^2$

Factor.

1. $x^2 - 18x + 81 =$ **$(x - 9)^2$**
2. $x^2 - 4x + 4 =$ **$(x - 2)^2$**
3. $x^2 - 16x + 64 =$ **$(x - 8)^2$**
4. $b^2 - 10b + 25 =$ **$(b - 5)^2$**
5. $x^2 + 14x + 49 =$ **$(x + 7)^2$**
6. $x^2 - 2x + 1 =$ **$(x - 1)^2$**
7. $c^2 - 6c + 9 =$ **$(c - 3)^2$**
8. $x^2 - 4xy + 4y^2 =$ **$(x - 2y)^2$**
9. $a^2 + 12ab + 36b^2 =$ **$(a + 6b)^2$**
10. $49x^2 + 28x + 4 =$ **$(7x + 2)^2$**
11. $x^2 + 14x + 49 =$ **$(x + 7)^2$**
12. $c^2 - 20c + 100 =$ **$(c - 10)^2$**
13. $y^2 - 22y + 121 =$ **$(y - 11)^2$**
14. $25a^2 - 40ab + 16b^2 =$ **$(5a - 4b)^2$**
15. $9x^2 - 12x + 4 =$ **$(3x - 2)^2$**
16. $16x^2 - 40x + 25 =$ **$(4x - 5)^2$**
17. $9x^2 + 12x + 4 =$ **$(3x + 2)^2$**
18. $x^2 - 14x + 49 =$ **$(x - 7)^2$**
19. $x^2 + 8x + 16 =$ **$(x + 4)^2$**
20. $4x^2 + 4x + 1 =$ **$(2x + 1)^2$**

Page 51 (bottom right)

Name _____ Date _____

Factoring

Factoring the Sum or Difference of Two Cubes

Rules: $x^3 + y^3 = (x + y)(x^2 - xy + y^2)$ $x^3 - y^3 = (x - y)(x^2 + xy + y^2)$
Examples: $x^3 + 8 = (x + 2)(x^2 - 2x + 4)$ $x^3 - 8 = (x - 2)(x^2 + 2x + 4)$

Factor.

1. $64x^3 + 1 =$ **$(4x + 1)(16x^2 - 4x + 1)$**
2. $8x^3 - 216 =$ **$8(x - 3)(x^2 + 3x + 9)$**
3. $8x^3 + 27 =$ **$(2x + 3)(4x^2 - 6x + 9)$**
4. $x^3 + y^3 =$ **$(x + y)(x^2 - xy + y^2)$**
5. $x^3 - 1000 =$ **$(x - 10)(x^2 + 10x + 100)$**
6. $1 - 64y^3 =$ **$(1 - 4y)(1 + 4y + 16y^2)$**
7. $x^3 + 125 =$ **$(x + 5)(x^2 - 5x + 25)$**
8. $x^3 - 27 =$ **$(x - 3)(x^2 + 3x + 9)$**
9. $x^3y^3 + 64 =$ **$(xy + 4)(x^2y^2 - 4xy + 16)$**
10. $64x^3 + 27y^3 =$ **$(4x + 3y)(16x^2 - 12xy + 9y^2)$**
11. $27x^3 + y^3 =$ **$(3x + y)(9x^2 - 3xy + y^2)$**
12. $x^3 - y^3 =$ **$(x - y)(x^2 + xy + y^2)$**
13. $27x^3 - 64 =$ **$(3x - 4)(9x^2 + 12x + 16)$**
14. $27x^3 - 27 =$ **$27(x - 1)(x^2 + x + 1)$**
15. $125a^3 - 8b^3 =$ **$(5a - 2b)(25a^2 + 10ab + 4b^2)$**
16. $64x^3 - y^3 =$ **$(4x - y)(16x^2 + 4xy + y^2)$**
17. $125x^3 - 64y^3 =$ **$(5x - 4y)(25x^2 + 20xy + 16y^2)$**
18. $64x^3 + 27 =$ **$(4x + 3)(16x^2 - 12x + 9)$**
19. $27x^3 - 8y^3 =$ **$(3x - 2y)(9x^2 + 6xy + 4y^2)$**
20. $x^3 - 8y^3 =$ **$(x - 2y)(x^2 + 2xy + 4y^2)$**

Name _____ Date _____

Factoring

Solving Equations by Factoring

The **Multiplication Property of Zero**: The product of a number and zero is zero.
The **Principle of Zero Products**: If the product of two factors is zero, then at least one of the factors must be zero. This principle is used in solving equations.

Solve: $(x - 4)(x - 5) = 0$ If $(x - 4)(x - 5) = 0$, then $(x - 4) = 0$ or $(x - 5) = 0$.

$x - 4 = 0$ $x - 5 = 0$ $x = 4$ $x = 5$
$x = 4$ $x = 5$ $(4 - 4)(4 - 5) = 0$ $(5 - 4)(5 - 5) = 0$
The solutions are 4 and 5. $(0)(-1) = 0$ $(1)(0) = 0$
                                      $0 = 0$ $0 = 0$

Write the solutions for each variable.

1. $x(x + 6) = 0$ **0, ⁻6**

2. $b^2 - 81 = 0$ **⁻9, 9**

3. $(27 - y)(y - 2) = 0$ **2, 27**

4. $z^2 - 1 = 0$ **⁻1, 1**

5. $(y - 4)(y - 8) = 0$ **4, 8**

6. $y(y - 11) = 0$ **0, 11**

7. $8t^2 - 32 = 0$ **2, ⁻2**

8. $x^2 - x - 6 = 0$ **⁻2, 3**

9. $x^2 - 4x - 21 = 0$ **⁻3, 7**

10. $m^2 - 144 = 0$ **⁻12, 12**

11. $(y + 5)(y + 6) = 0$ **⁻5, ⁻6**

12. $(2x + 4)(x + 7) = 0$ **⁻7, ⁻2**

13. $z^2 - 9 = 0$ **⁻3, 3**

14. $10x^2 - 10x = 0$ **1, 0**

15. $2x^2 - 6x = x - 3$ **$\frac{1}{2}$, 3**

16. $4y(3y - 2) = 0$ **0, $\frac{2}{3}$**

17. $(4y - 1)(y + 2) = 0$ **$\frac{1}{4}$, ⁻2**

18. $x^2 - 5x + 6 = 0$ **2, 3**

52   CD-104316 • © Carson-Dellosa

Name _____ Date _____

Factoring

Problem Solving

The length of a rectangle is 5 inches longer than the width. The area of the rectangle is 50 square inches. Find the length and width of the rectangle.

Width of rectangle: w
Length of rectangle: $w + 5$
$A = lw$
$50 = (w + 5)(w)$ Since the width cannot be a negative number,
$50 = w^2 + 5w$ the width is 5.
$0 = w^2 + 5w - 50$
$0 = (w + 10)(w - 5)$ $l = 5 + 5 = 10$
$w + 10 = 0$ or $w - 5 = 0$
$w = ⁻10$ $w = 5$ The length is 10, and the width is 5.

For each word problem, write an equation and solve it.

1. The sum of twice a number and its square is 143. Find the numbers.

Equation **$2x + x^2 = 143$**   Solution **$x = ⁻13, 11$**

2. The sum of a number and its square is 42. Find the numbers.

Equation **$x + x^2 = 42$**   Solution **$x = ⁻7, 6$**

3. The sum of a number and its square is 56. Find the numbers.

Equation **$x + x^2 = 56$**   Solution **$x = ⁻8, 7$**

4. The sum of a number and its square is 90. Find the numbers.

Equation **$x + x^2 = 90$**   Solution **$x = ⁻10, 9$**

5. The square of a number is 80 more than 2 times the number. Find the numbers.

Equation **$x^2 = 2x + 80$**   Solution **$x = 10, ⁻8$**

6. The square of a number is 48 more than 2 times the number. Find the numbers.

Equation **$x^2 = 2x + 48$**   Solution **$x = 8, ⁻6$**

7. For what numbers is the sum of a number and its square equal to 110?

Equation **$x + x^2 = 110$**   Solution **$x = ⁻11, 10$**

CD-104316 • © Carson-Dellosa   53

Name _____ Date _____

Factoring

Problem Solving

The length of a rectangle is 3 inches longer than the width. The area of the rectangle is 40 square inches. Find the length and width of the rectangle.

Width of rectangle: w
Length of rectangle: $w + 3$
$A = lw$
$40 = (w + 3)(w)$ Since the width cannot be a negative number,
$40 = w^2 + 3w$ the width is 5.
$0 = w^2 + 3w - 40$
$0 = (w + 8)(w - 5)$ $l = 5 + 3 = 8$
$w + 8 = 0$ or $w - 5 = 0$
$w = ⁻8$ $w = 5$ The length is 8, and the width is 5.

For each word problem, write an equation and solve it.

1. The area of a square is 121 m². Find the length of the sides of the square.

Equation **$s^2 = 121$**   Solution **$s = 11$**

2. The area of a rectangle is 72 m². Its length is twice its width. Find the length and width of the rectangle.

Equation **$2w^2 = 72$**   Solution **$l = 12, w = 6$**

3. The area of a rectangle is 36 cm². Its width is 4 times its length. Find the length and width of the rectangle.

Equation **$4l^2 = 36$**   Solution **$l = 3, w = 12$**

4. The width of a rectangle is 5 more than twice its length. The area of the rectangle is 33 in.². Find the dimensions of the rectangle.

Equation **$2l^2 + 5l = 33$**   Solution **$l = 3, w = 11$**

5. The length of a rectangle is 4 more than twice its width. The area of the rectangle is 96 ft.². Find its dimensions.

Equation **$2w^2 + 4w = 96$**   Solution **$l = 16, w = 6$**

54   CD-104316 • © Carson-Dellosa

Name _____ Date _____

Rational Expressions

Dividing Monomials

$$\frac{35x^9y^6}{5x^7y^8} = \frac{35}{5} \cdot x^{9-7}\, y^{6-8} = \frac{7x^2}{y^2}$$

Simplify.

1. $\frac{a^3}{a^5}$ **$\frac{1}{a^2}$**

2. $\frac{a^5b^2}{2a^2}$ **$\frac{a^3b^2}{2}$**

3. $\frac{13m^6n^7}{39m^3n^5}$ **$\frac{m^3n^2}{3}$**

4. $\frac{9x^8y^7z^8}{18x^5y^5z^4}$ **$\frac{x^3y^2z^4}{2}$**

5. $\frac{7c^2d^3}{28cd^2}$ **$\frac{cd}{4}$**

6. $\frac{10a^6b^8}{40a^2b^2}$ **$\frac{a^4b^6}{4}$**

7. $\frac{18a^8b^2c^6}{36a^4bc^2}$ **$\frac{a^2bc^4}{2}$**

8. $\frac{5x^3y^2z^2}{5x^2yz}$ **xyz**

9. $\frac{45x^9y^{10}z^5}{51x^9y^8z^3}$ **$\frac{15y^2z^2}{17}$**

10. $\frac{16x^2y^4}{4x^2y^3}$ **$4y$**

11. $\frac{18x^6y^3z^4}{12x^3y^2z^3}$ **$\frac{3x^3yz}{2}$**

12. $\frac{72x^5y^5z^6}{8x^4yz^3}$ **$9xy^4z^3$**

13. $\frac{18a^9b^3}{54a^2b^2}$ **$\frac{a^7b}{3}$**

14. $\frac{44x^8y^2}{11x^7yz}$ **$\frac{4xy}{z}$**

CD-104316 • © Carson-Dellosa   55

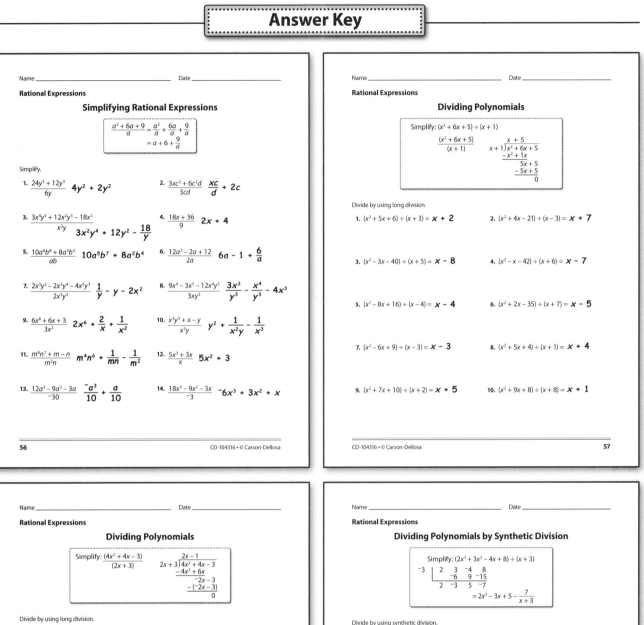

Page 56 (left):

Name _____ Date _____

Rational Expressions

Simplifying Rational Expressions

$$\frac{a^2 + 6a + 9}{a} = \frac{a^2}{a} + \frac{6a}{a} + \frac{9}{a}$$
$$= a + 6 + \frac{9}{a}$$

Simplify.

1. $\frac{24y^5 + 12y^3}{6y}$ **$4y^2 + 2y^2$**

2. $\frac{3xc^2 + 6c^2d}{3cd}$ **$\frac{xc}{d} + 2c$**

3. $\frac{3x^4y^5 + 12x^2y^3 - 18x^2}{x^2y}$ **$3x^2y^4 + 12y^2 - \frac{18}{y}$**

4. $\frac{18x + 36}{9}$ **$2x + 4$**

5. $\frac{10a^6b^8 + 8a^3b^5}{ab}$ **$10a^5b^7 + 8a^2b^4$**

6. $\frac{12a^2 - 2a + 12}{2a}$ **$6a - 1 + \frac{6}{a}$**

7. $\frac{2x^3y^2 - 2x^3y^4 - 4x^5y^3}{2x^3y^3}$ **$\frac{1}{y} - y - 2x^2$**

8. $\frac{9y^4 - 3x^5 - 12x^4y^3}{3xy^3}$ **$\frac{3x^3}{y^3} - \frac{x^4}{y^3} - 4x^3$**

9. $\frac{6x^8 + 6x + 3}{3x^2}$ **$2x^6 + \frac{2}{x} + \frac{1}{x^2}$**

10. $\frac{x^3y^3 + x - y}{x^3y}$ **$y^2 + \frac{1}{x^2y} - \frac{1}{x^3}$**

11. $\frac{m^6n^7 + m - n}{m^2n}$ **$m^4n^6 + \frac{1}{mn} - \frac{1}{m^2}$**

12. $\frac{5x^3 + 3x}{x}$ **$5x^2 + 3$**

13. $\frac{12a^3 - 9a^3 - 3a}{-30}$ **$\frac{-a^3}{10} + \frac{a}{10}$**

14. $\frac{18x^3 - 9x^2 - 3x}{-3}$ **$-6x^3 + 3x^2 + x$**

56   CD-104316 • © Carson-Dellosa

Page 57 (right):

Name _____ Date _____

Rational Expressions

Dividing Polynomials

Simplify: $(x^2 + 6x + 5) \div (x + 1)$

$$\frac{(x^2 + 6x + 5)}{(x + 1)}$$

$$\begin{array}{r} x + 5 \\ x+1\overline{)x^2 + 6x + 5} \\ \underline{-x^2 + 1x} \\ 5x + 5 \\ \underline{-5x + 5} \\ 0 \end{array}$$

Divide by using long division.

1. $(x^2 + 5x + 6) \div (x + 3) =$ **$x + 2$**

2. $(x^2 + 4x - 21) \div (x - 3) =$ **$x + 7$**

3. $(x^2 - 3x - 40) \div (x + 5) =$ **$x - 8$**

4. $(x^2 - x - 42) \div (x + 6) =$ **$x - 7$**

5. $(x^2 - 8x + 16) \div (x - 4) =$ **$x - 4$**

6. $(x^2 + 2x - 35) \div (x + 7) =$ **$x - 5$**

7. $(x^2 - 6x + 9) \div (x - 3) =$ **$x - 3$**

8. $(x^2 + 5x + 4) \div (x + 1) =$ **$x + 4$**

9. $(x^2 + 7x + 10) \div (x + 2) =$ **$x + 5$**

10. $(x^2 + 9x + 8) \div (x + 8) =$ **$x + 1$**

CD-104316 • © Carson-Dellosa   57

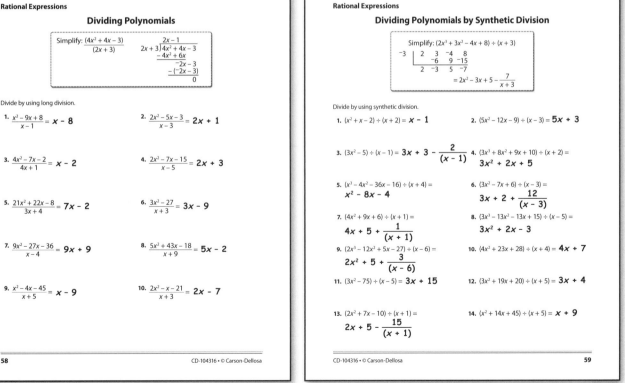

Page 58 (left):

Name _____ Date _____

Rational Expressions

Dividing Polynomials

Simplify: $\frac{(4x^2 + 4x - 3)}{(2x + 3)}$

$$\begin{array}{r} 2x - 1 \\ 2x+3\overline{)4x^2 + 4x - 3} \\ \underline{-4x^2 + 6x} \\ -2x - 3 \\ \underline{-(-2x - 3)} \\ 0 \end{array}$$

Divide by using long division.

1. $\frac{x^2 - 9x + 8}{x - 1} =$ **$x - 8$**

2. $\frac{2x^2 - 5x - 3}{x - 3} =$ **$2x + 1$**

3. $\frac{4x^2 - 7x - 2}{4x + 1} =$ **$x - 2$**

4. $\frac{2x^2 - 7x - 15}{x - 5} =$ **$2x + 3$**

5. $\frac{21x^2 + 22x - 8}{3x + 4} =$ **$7x - 2$**

6. $\frac{3x^2 - 27}{x + 3} =$ **$3x - 9$**

7. $\frac{9x^2 - 27x - 36}{x - 4} =$ **$9x + 9$**

8. $\frac{5x^2 + 43x - 18}{x + 9} =$ **$5x - 2$**

9. $\frac{x^2 - 4x - 45}{x + 5} =$ **$x - 9$**

10. $\frac{2x^2 - x - 21}{x + 3} =$ **$2x - 7$**

58   CD-104316 • © Carson-Dellosa

Page 59 (right):

Name _____ Date _____

Rational Expressions

Dividing Polynomials by Synthetic Division

Simplify: $(2x^3 + 3x^2 - 4x + 8) \div (x + 3)$

$$\begin{array}{r|rrrr} -3 & 2 & 3 & -4 & 8 \\ & & -6 & 9 & -15 \\ \hline & 2 & -3 & 5 & -7 \end{array}$$

$$= 2x^2 - 3x + 5 - \frac{7}{x + 3}$$

Divide by using synthetic division.

1. $(x^2 + x - 2) \div (x + 2) =$ **$x - 1$**

2. $(5x^2 - 12x - 9) \div (x - 3) =$ **$5x + 3$**

3. $(3x^2 - 5) \div (x - 1) =$ **$3x + 3 - \frac{2}{(x - 1)}$**

4. $(3x^3 + 8x^2 + 9x + 10) \div (x + 2) =$ **$3x^2 + 2x + 5$**

5. $(x^3 - 4x^2 - 36x - 16) \div (x + 4) =$ **$x^2 - 8x - 4$**

6. $(3x^2 - 7x + 6) \div (x - 3) =$ **$3x + 2 + \frac{12}{(x - 3)}$**

7. $(4x^2 + 9x + 6) \div (x + 1) =$ **$4x + 5 + \frac{1}{(x + 1)}$**

8. $(3x^3 - 13x^2 - 13x + 15) \div (x - 5) =$ **$3x^2 + 2x - 3$**

9. $(2x^3 - 12x^2 + 5x - 27) \div (x - 6) =$ **$2x^2 + 5 + \frac{3}{(x - 6)}$**

10. $(4x^2 + 23x + 28) \div (x + 4) =$ **$4x + 7$**

11. $(3x^2 - 75) \div (x - 5) =$ **$3x + 15$**

12. $(3x^2 + 19x + 20) \div (x + 5) =$ **$3x + 4$**

13. $(2x^2 + 7x - 10) \div (x + 1) =$ **$2x + 5 - \frac{15}{(x + 1)}$**

14. $(x^2 + 14x + 45) \div (x + 5) =$ **$x + 9$**

CD-104316 • © Carson-Dellosa   59

Name _____ Date _____

Rational Expressions

Multiplying Rational Expressions

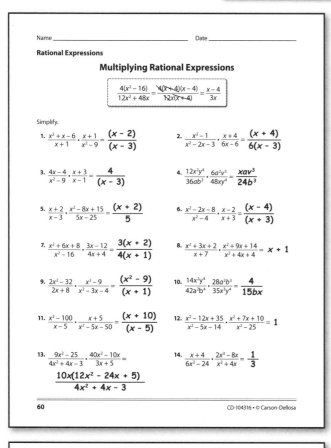

$$\frac{4(x^2-16)}{12x^2+48x} = \frac{4(x+4)(x-4)}{12x(x+4)} = \frac{x-4}{3x}$$

Simplify.

1. $\frac{x^2+x-6}{x+1} \cdot \frac{x+1}{x^2-9} = \frac{(x-2)}{(x-3)}$

2. $\frac{x^2-1}{x^2-2x-3} \cdot \frac{x+4}{6x-6} = \frac{(x+4)}{6(x-3)}$

3. $\frac{4x-4}{x^2-9} \cdot \frac{x+3}{x-1} = \frac{4}{(x-3)}$

4. $\frac{12x^3y^4}{36ab^3} \cdot \frac{6a^2v^3}{48xy^4} = \frac{xav^3}{24b^3}$

5. $\frac{x+2}{x-3} \cdot \frac{x^2-8x+15}{5x-25} = \frac{(x+2)}{5}$

6. $\frac{x^2-2x-8}{x^2-4} \cdot \frac{x-2}{x+3} = \frac{(x-4)}{(x+3)}$

7. $\frac{x^2+6x+8}{x^2-16} \cdot \frac{3x-12}{4x+4} = \frac{3(x+2)}{4(x+1)}$

8. $\frac{x^2+3x+2}{x+7} \cdot \frac{x^2+9x+14}{x^2+4x+4} = x+1$

9. $\frac{2x^2-32}{2x+8} \cdot \frac{x^2-9}{x^2-3x-4} = \frac{(x^2-9)}{(x+1)}$

10. $\frac{14x^3y^4}{42a^2b^4} \cdot \frac{28a^2b^3}{35x^3y^4} = \frac{4}{15bx}$

11. $\frac{x^2-100}{x-5} \cdot \frac{x+5}{x^2-5x-50} = \frac{(x+10)}{(x-5)}$

12. $\frac{x^2-12x+35}{x^2-5x-14} \cdot \frac{x^2+7x+10}{x^2-25} = 1$

13. $\frac{9x^2-25}{4x^2+4x-3} \cdot \frac{40x^2-10x}{3x+5} =$

$$\frac{10x(12x^2-24x+5)}{4x^2+4x-3}$$

14. $\frac{x+4}{6x^2-24} \cdot \frac{2x^3-8x}{x^2+4x} = \frac{1}{3}$

CD-104316 • © Carson-Dellosa

Name _____ Date _____

Rational Expressions

Dividing Rational Expressions

Simplify.

1. $\frac{x-7}{x+2} \div \frac{x^2-49}{x^2+9x+14} = 1$

2. $\frac{x+2}{4x(x-6)} \div \frac{x^2-4}{8x(x-6)} = \frac{2}{(x-2)}$

3. $\frac{x^2-4}{4x+4} \div \frac{x-2}{x+1} = \frac{(x+2)}{4}$

4. $\frac{x+2}{x+3} \div \frac{x^2-4}{x-2} = \frac{1}{(x+3)}$

5. $\frac{2x^2+12x+18}{x^2+5x-6} \div \frac{2x+6}{x-1} = \frac{(x+3)}{(x+6)}$

6. $\frac{2x^2+6x}{x^2+2x} \div \frac{x^2-9}{4x-12} = \frac{8}{(x+2)}$

7. $\frac{15x^4y^2}{5xy} \div \frac{10x^3y}{5y^2} = \frac{3y^2}{2}$

8. $\frac{x^2+8x}{x^2+14x+48} \div \frac{x^2+x}{x^2} = \frac{x^2}{x^2+7x+6}$

9. $\frac{3x^2+6x}{x^2+6x} \div \frac{x^2-4}{2x-4} = \frac{6}{(x+6)}$

10. $\frac{x^2-16}{x^2+7x+12} \div \frac{5x-20}{x+3} = \frac{1}{5}$

11. $\frac{x^2-7x}{x^2-14x+49} \div \frac{2x^2+6x}{x^2+x-56} = \frac{x+8}{2(x+3)}$

12. $\frac{x^2+9x-10}{x^2+5x-14} \div \frac{3x+30}{2x-4} = \frac{(2x-2)}{(3x+21)}$

13. $\frac{27x^6y^2}{9x^3y} \div \frac{4x^5y^3}{16x^4y^2} = 12x^2$

14. $\frac{24a^4b^2}{8a^2b} \div \frac{12ab^3}{16a^3b} = \frac{4a^2}{b}$

CD-104316 • © Carson-Dellosa

Name _____ Date _____

Rational Expressions

Adding and Subtracting Rational Expressions

$$\frac{7x-12}{2x^2+5x-12} - \frac{3x-6}{2x^2+5x-12} = \frac{(7x-12)-(3x-6)}{2x^2+5x-12} = \frac{7x-12-3x+6}{2x^2+5x-12} =$$

$$\frac{2(2x-3)}{(2x-3)(x+4)} = \frac{2(2x-3)}{(2x-3)(x+4)} = \frac{2}{x+4}$$

Simplify.

1. $\frac{2}{x+2} + \frac{6x}{x^2-4} = \frac{8x-4}{[(x-2)(x+2)]}$

2. $\frac{7a}{a-4} + \frac{5}{a+4} = \frac{7a^2+33a-20}{[(a+4)(a-4)]}$

3. $\frac{3}{4xy} + \frac{14}{3xy} - \frac{9}{2xy} = \frac{11}{12xy}$

4. $\frac{x}{2x-5} + \frac{3}{2x-5} = \frac{(3+x)}{(2x-5)}$

5. $\frac{x}{x-4} + \frac{4}{x^2-x-12} = \frac{(x^2+3x+4)}{[(x-4)(x+3)]}$

6. $\frac{4}{3x-8} - \frac{x}{4x-7} = \frac{(^-3x^2+24x-28)}{[(4x-7)(3x-8)]}$

7. $-\frac{4}{2x^2} + \frac{5}{2x^2} + \frac{8}{3x^2} = \frac{19}{6x^2}$

8. $-\frac{4x}{x^2+x-2} + \frac{4x}{x^2+x-2} = 0$

9. $\frac{11x}{x^2-6x-7} + \frac{5x}{x^2+9x+8} =$

$$\frac{(16x^2+53)}{[(x-7)(x+1)(x+8)]}$$

10. $\frac{3x}{x^2-4} + \frac{5x}{x^2-4} = \frac{8x}{[(x+2)(x-2)]}$

11. $-\frac{10}{4x^2} + \frac{6}{4x^2} + \frac{8}{4x^2} =$

$$\frac{1}{x^2}$$

12. $\frac{5}{2xy} + \frac{5}{4xy} - \frac{12}{6xy} = \frac{7}{4xy}$

CD-104316 • © Carson-Dellosa

Name _____ Date _____

Rational Expressions

Solving Fractional Equations

$\frac{3}{6} + \frac{8x}{12} = \frac{5}{2}$ → Multiply both sides of the equation by the LCD to eliminate all denominators.

$12(\frac{3}{6} + \frac{8x}{12}) = 12(\frac{5}{2})$ → $\frac{36}{6} + \frac{96x}{12} = \frac{60}{2}$

$6 + 8x = 30$ → $6 - 6 + 8x = 30 - 6$ → $8x = 24$ → $x = 3$

Solve.

1. $\frac{2}{17} = \frac{x-6}{x+9}$ $x = 8$

2. $\frac{3}{4} = \frac{x+2}{x-8}$ $x = {}^-32$

3. $1 - \frac{4}{y} = 5$ $y = {}^-1$

4. $\frac{6}{x} - \frac{2}{8} = \frac{x}{8}$ $x = 6, {}^-8$

5. $\frac{x}{2} + \frac{5}{6} = \frac{x}{3}$ $x = {}^-5$

6. $\frac{(x-4)}{30} = \frac{1}{5}$ $x = 10$

7. $17 - \frac{3}{x} = 8$ $x = \frac{1}{3}$

8. $\frac{x+2}{x+7} = \frac{7}{12}$ $x = 5$

9. $\frac{6}{(x+4)} = \frac{x-3}{22-x}$ $x = 9, {}^-16$

10. $\frac{x+1}{x+5} = \frac{5}{9}$ $x = 4$

11. $\frac{x+7}{x-9} = \frac{28}{12}$ $x = 21$

12. $\frac{x-5}{x-1} = \frac{1}{5}$ $x = 6$

13. $\frac{x-2}{x+6} = \frac{1}{9}$ $x = 3$

14. $3 - \frac{9}{y} = 30$ $y = -\frac{1}{3}$

CD-104316 • © Carson-Dellosa

CD-104316 • © Carson-Dellosa

Name _____ Date _____

Ratios and Proportions

Proportions

Solve the following ratio for *x*.

$\frac{x}{5} = \frac{4}{10}$ → Take cross products and solve. → $\frac{x}{5} \times \frac{4}{10}$ → $5 \cdot 4 = 20$, $x \cdot 10 = 10x$

→ $10x = 20$ → $\frac{10x}{10} = \frac{20}{10}$ → $x = 2$

Solve.

1. $\frac{4}{(x-3)} = \frac{28}{49}$ $x = 10$

2. $\frac{(5+x)}{10} = \frac{2}{5}$ $x = {}^-1$

3. $\frac{x}{30} = \frac{7}{10}$ $x = 21$

4. $\frac{(x-2)}{16} = \frac{x}{4}$ $x = {}^-\frac{2}{3}$

5. $\frac{2}{x} = \frac{6}{30}$ $x = 10$

6. $\frac{(x+1)}{7} = \frac{6}{14}$ $x = 2$

7. $\frac{x}{15} = \frac{5}{75}$ $x = 1$

8. $\frac{x}{20} = \frac{2}{10}$ $x = 4$

9. $\frac{x}{6} = \frac{(x-3)}{12}$ $x = {}^-3$

10. $\frac{x}{5} = \frac{12}{6}$ $x = 10$

11. $\frac{6}{(x+5)} = \frac{18}{24}$ $x = 3$

12. $\frac{5}{15} = \frac{x}{9}$ $x = 3$

13. $\frac{x+x}{10} = \frac{5}{2}$ $x = \frac{25}{2}$

14. $\frac{x}{3} = \frac{12}{27}$ $x = \frac{4}{3}$

64   CD-104316 • © Carson-Dellosa

Name _____ Date _____

Ratios and Proportions

Problem Solving with Proportions

Three liters of soda cost $3.00. At this rate, how much would 10 liters of soda cost? *To find the cost, write and solve a ratio using x to represent the cost.*

$\frac{\text{liters}}{\text{cost}}$ → $\frac{3}{3.00} = \frac{10}{x}$ → $3x = 10(3.00)$ → $3x = 30$ → $\frac{3x}{3} = \frac{30}{3}$

→ $x = 10$ → The cost of 10 liters of soda is $10.00.

Solve.

1. The real estate tax for a house that costs $56,000 is $1,400. At this rate, what is the value of a house for which the real estate tax is $1,800?

$\frac{\text{value}}{\text{tax}} = \frac{\$56,000}{\$1,400} = \frac{x}{\$1,800} =$ value = $72,000

2. A copy machine can print 120 pages per minute. At this rate, how many minutes are required to make 840 copies?

$\frac{\text{copies}}{\text{minute}} = \frac{1}{120} = \frac{x}{840} =$ minutes = 7 minutes

3. One hundred thirty-six tiles are required to tile a 36 ft.² area. At this rate, how many tiles are required to tile a 288 ft.² area?

$\frac{\text{tiles}}{\text{area}} = \frac{136}{36} = \frac{x}{288} =$ tiles = 1,088 tiles

4. Two gallons of fruit juice will serve 35 people. How much fruit juice is necessary to serve 105 people?

$\frac{\text{gallons}}{\text{people}} = \frac{2}{25} = \frac{x}{105} =$ gallons = 6 gallons

5. A stock investment of $4,000 earns $360 each year. At the same rate, how much money can a person earn if he invests $6,000?

$\frac{\text{interest}}{\text{investment}} = \frac{\$360}{\$4,000} = \frac{x}{\$6,000} =$ interest = $540

CD-104316 • © Carson-Dellosa   65

Name _____ Date _____

Ratios and Proportions

Problem Solving with Proportions

Three gallons of gasoline costs $3.00. At this rate, how much would 6 gallons of gasoline cost? *To find the cost, write and solve a proportion using x to represent the cost.*

$\frac{\text{gallons}}{\text{cost}}$ → $\frac{3}{\$3} = \frac{6}{x}$ → $3x = 18$ → $\frac{3x}{3} = \frac{18}{3}$ → $x = 6$

→ The cost of 6 gallons of gasoline is $6.00.

Solve.

1. An investment of $36,000 earns $900 each year. At the same rate, how much money must be invested to earn $1,200 each year?

$\frac{\text{investment}}{\text{earning}} = \frac{\$36,000}{\$900} = \frac{x}{\$1,200} =$ investment = $48,000

2. The sales tax on a $15,000 car is $540. At this rate, what is the tax on a $32,000 car?

$\frac{\text{tax}}{\text{value}} = \frac{\$540}{\$15,000} = \frac{x}{\$32,000} =$ tax = $1,152

3. Six gallons of paint will cover 120 doors. At this rate, how many gallons of paint are needed to cover 480 doors?

$\frac{\text{gallons}}{\text{doors}} = \frac{6}{120} = \frac{x}{480} =$ gallons = 24 gallons

4. A lawnmower can cut 1 acre on 0.5 gallons of gasoline. At this rate, how much gasoline is needed to cut 3.5 acres?

$\frac{\text{gallons}}{\text{acres}} = \frac{0.5}{1} = \frac{x}{3.5} =$ gallons = 1.75 gallons

5. An aerobics instructor burns 400 calories in 1 hour. How many hours would the instructor have to do aerobics to burn 660 calories?

$\frac{\text{hours}}{\text{calories}} = \frac{1}{400} = \frac{x}{660} =$ 1.65 hours

66   CD-104316 • © Carson-Dellosa

Name _____ Date _____

Graphing

Graphing Ordered Pairs

Start at the origin (0, 0).
$(x, y) = (1, {}^-2)$ right 1 and down 2
$(x, y) = ({}^-3, 4)$ left 3 and up 4
$(x, y) = (2, {}^-2)$ right 2 and down 2

Label the following points.
Start at the origin (0, 0).

A (6, 2)
B (6, 3)
C (5, 1)
D (5, 0)
E (1, ⁻3)
F (2, ⁻6)
G (5, 4)
H (2, 4)
I (4, 3)
J (1, ⁻2)
K (5, ⁻3)
L (1, 4)
M (3, 1)

CD-104316 • © Carson-Dellosa   67

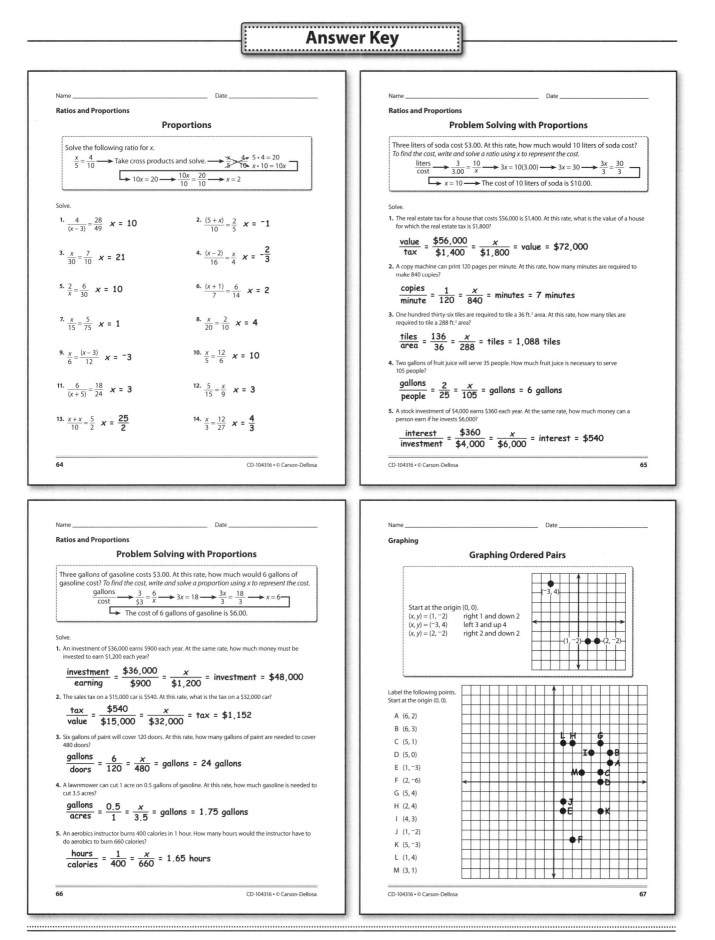

Page 68

Name _____ Date _____

Graphing

Graphing Ordered Pairs

Start at the origin (0, 0).
$(x, y) = (1, ^-2)$ right 1 and down 2
$(x, y) = (^-3, 4)$ left 3 and up 4
$(x, y) = (2, ^-2)$ right 2 and down 2

(−3, 4)
(1, −2) (2, −2)

Label the following points.
Start at the origin (0, 0).

A $(^-1, 2)$
B $(^-1, 0)$
C $(^-1, ^-6)$
D $(^-4, 2)$
E $(^-6, 2)$
F $(^-5, 6)$
G $(^-4, 1)$
H $(2, ^-8)$
I $(6, 6)$
J $(^-7, 5)$
K $(^-1, ^-1)$
L $(^-3, ^-3)$
M $(6, ^-4)$

Page 69

Name _____ Date _____

Graphing

Plotting Points

$y - 3 = 4x$
$y - 3 + 3 = 4x + 3$
$y = 4x + 3$

Let $x = ^-2, 1, 2$
Solve for y.

$x = ^-2$	$x = 1$	$x = 2$
$y = 4 \cdot ^-2 + 3$	$y = 4 \cdot 1 + 3$	$y = 4 \cdot 2 + 3$
$y = ^-8 + 3$	$y = 4 + 3$	$y = 8 + 3$
$y = ^-5$	$y = 7$	$y = 11$
$(^-2, ^-5)$	$(1, 7)$	$(2, 11)$

Solve each equation for y. Use the given values for x to find the values for y. Write answers as ordered pairs.

1. $6x - y = ^-18$ Let $x = 2, 3, ^-2$
$(2, 30) (3, 36) (^-2, 6)$

2. $^-x = y - 8$ Let $x = ^-1, ^-2, 1$
$(^-1, 9) (^-2, 10) (1, 7)$

3. $2x + y = ^-4$ Let $x = ^-3, 2, 4$
$(^-3, 2) (2, ^-8) (4, ^-12)$

4. $6x + y = 3$ Let $x = ^-4, 0, 2$
$(^-4, 27) (0, 3) (2, ^-9)$

5. $4 - y = 3x$ Let $x = ^-3, 1, ^-2$
$(^-3, 13) (1, 1) (^-2, 10)$

6. $2 = y - 6x$ Let $x = ^-1, 0, 2$
$(^-1, ^-4) (0, 2) (2, 14)$

7. $2x + y = ^-12$ Let $x = ^-2, 0, 3$
$(^-2, ^-8) (0, ^-12) (3, ^-18)$

Page 70

Name _____ Date _____

Graphing

Graphing Ordered Pairs

Solve for y in each equation. Choose 3 values for x and find the values for y.
Graph the 3 ordered pairs and draw a line connecting them.

$y - 3 = 2x$
$y - 3 + 3 = 2x + 3$
$y = 2x + 3$

x	y
$^-2$	$^-1$
0	3
1	5

$y = 2 \cdot ^-2 + 3$ $y = 2 \cdot 0 + 3$ $y = 2 \cdot 1 + 3$
$y = ^-4 + 3$ $y = 0 + 3$ $y = 2 + 3$
$y = ^-1$ $y = 3$ $y = 5$

Page 71

Name _____ Date _____

Graphing

Graphing Linear Equations

Graph each equation by plotting points.

1. $x + y = 4$

x	y
4	0
5	$^-1$
6	$^-2$

2. $y = 3 - x$

x	y
5	$^-2$
$^-2$	5
0	3

3. $4x + y = 6$

x	y
0	6
1	2
2	$^-2$

4. $y = 2x - 7$

x	y
3	$^-1$
4	1
5	3

5. $y = x + 3$

x	y
2	5
0	3
$^-3$	0

6. $y = 9 - x$

x	y
0	9
4	5
3	6

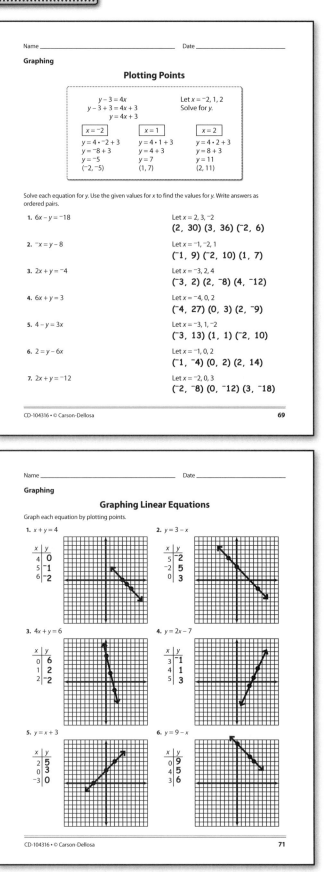

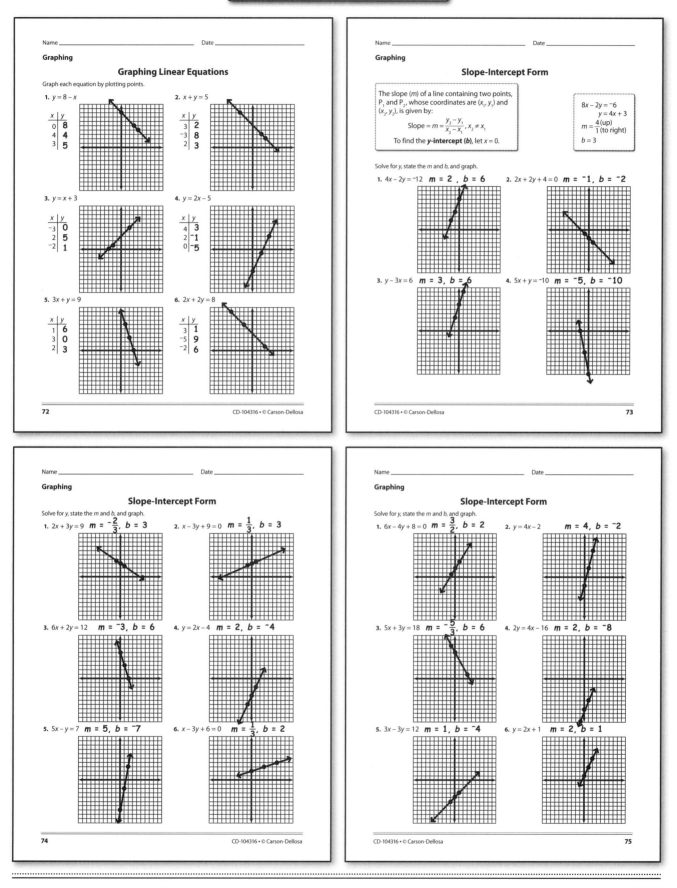

Name _____ Date _____

Graphing

Graphing Linear Equations

Graph each equation by plotting points.

1. $y = 8 - x$

x	y
0	8
4	4
3	5

2. $x + y = 5$

x	y
3	2
-3	8
2	3

3. $y = x + 3$

x	y
-3	0
2	5
-2	1

4. $y = 2x - 5$

x	y
4	3
2	-1
0	-5

5. $3x + y = 9$

x	y
1	6
3	0
2	3

6. $2x + 2y = 8$

x	y
3	1
-5	9
-2	6

72   CD-104316 • © Carson-Dellosa

Name _____ Date _____

Graphing

Slope-Intercept Form

The slope (m) of a line containing two points, P_1 and P_2, whose coordinates are (x_1, y_1) and (x_2, y_2), is given by:

Slope = $m = \dfrac{y_2 - y_1}{x_2 - x_1}$, $x_2 \neq x_1$

To find the **y-intercept (b)**, let $x = 0$.

$8x - 2y = ^-6$
$y = 4x + 3$
$m = \dfrac{4}{1}$ (up) (to right)
$b = 3$

Solve for y, state the m and b, and graph.

1. $4x - 2y = ^-12$ $m = 2$, $b = 6$

2. $2x + 2y + 4 = 0$ $m = ^-1$, $b = ^-2$

3. $y - 3x = 6$ $m = 3$, $b = 6$

4. $5x + y = ^-10$ $m = ^-5$, $b = ^-10$

CD-104316 • © Carson-Dellosa   73

Name _____ Date _____

Graphing

Slope-Intercept Form

Solve for y, state the m and b, and graph.

1. $2x + 3y = 9$ $m = ^-\dfrac{2}{3}$, $b = 3$

2. $x - 3y + 9 = 0$ $m = \dfrac{1}{3}$, $b = 3$

3. $6x + 2y = 12$ $m = ^-3$, $b = 6$

4. $y = 2x - 4$ $m = 2$, $b = ^-4$

5. $5x - y = 7$ $m = 5$, $b = ^-7$

6. $x - 3y + 6 = 0$ $m = \dfrac{1}{3}$, $b = 2$

74   CD-104316 • © Carson-Dellosa

Name _____ Date _____

Graphing

Slope-Intercept Form

Solve for y, state the m and b, and graph.

1. $6x - 4y + 8 = 0$ $m = \dfrac{3}{2}$, $b = 2$

2. $y = 4x - 2$ $m = 4$, $b = ^-2$

3. $5x + 3y = 18$ $m = ^-\dfrac{5}{3}$, $b = 6$

4. $2y = 4x - 16$ $m = 2$, $b = ^-8$

5. $3x - 3y = 12$ $m = 1$, $b = ^-4$

6. $y = 2x + 1$ $m = 2$, $b = 1$

CD-104316 • © Carson-Dellosa   75

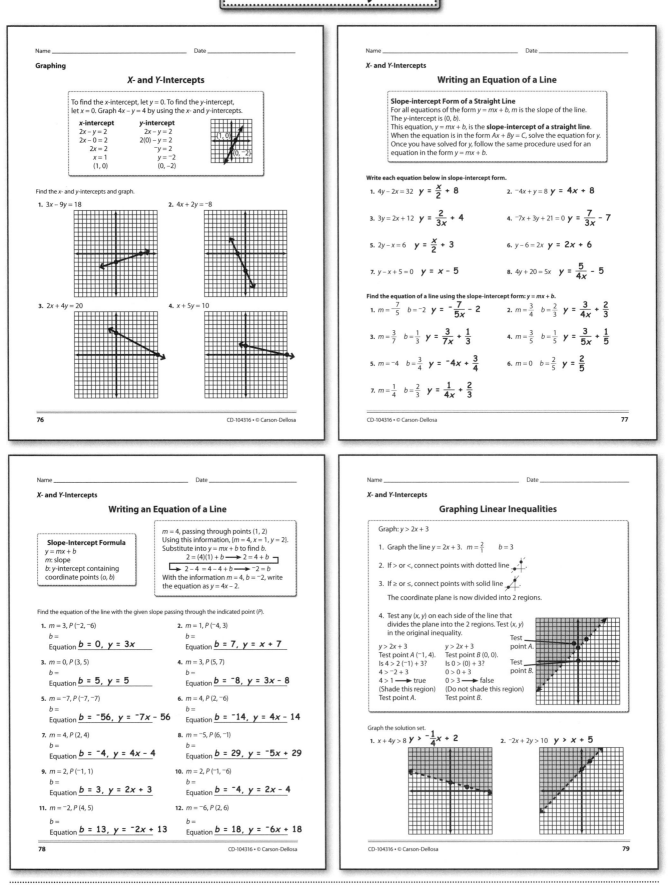

Graphing

X- and Y-Intercepts

To find the x-intercept, let y = 0. To find the y-intercept, let x = 0. Graph 4x – y = 4 by using the x- and y-intercepts.

x-intercept	y-intercept
2x – y = 2	2x – y = 2
2x – 0 = 2	2(0) – y = 2
2x = 2	⁻y = 2
x = 1	y = ⁻2
(1, 0)	(0, ⁻2)

Find the x- and y-intercepts and graph.

1. 3x – 9y = 18

2. 4x + 2y = ⁻8

3. 2x + 4y = 20

4. x + 5y = 10

CD-104316 • © Carson-Dellosa

X- and Y-Intercepts

Writing an Equation of a Line

Slope-intercept Form of a Straight Line
For all equations of the form y = mx + b, m is the slope of the line. The y-intercept is (0, b).
This equation, y = mx + b, is the **slope-intercept of a straight line**.
When the equation is in the form Ax + By = C, solve the equation for y. Once you have solved for y, follow the same procedure used for an equation in the form y = mx + b.

Write each equation below in slope-intercept form.

1. $4y - 2x = 32$ $y = \frac{x}{2} + 8$

2. $^-4x + y = 8$ $y = 4x + 8$

3. $3y = 2x + 12$ $y = \frac{2}{3x} + 4$

4. $^-7x + 3y + 21 = 0$ $y = \frac{7}{3x} - 7$

5. $2y - x = 6$ $y = \frac{x}{2} + 3$

6. $y - 6 = 2x$ $y = 2x + 6$

7. $y - x + 5 = 0$ $y = x - 5$

8. $4y + 20 = 5x$ $y = \frac{5}{4x} - 5$

Find the equation of a line using the slope-intercept form: y = mx + b.

1. $m = \frac{7}{5}$ $b = ^-2$ $y = ^-\frac{7}{5x} - 2$

2. $m = \frac{3}{4}$ $b = \frac{2}{3}$ $y = \frac{3}{4x} + \frac{2}{3}$

3. $m = \frac{3}{7}$ $b = \frac{1}{3}$ $y = \frac{3}{7x} + \frac{1}{3}$

4. $m = \frac{3}{5}$ $b = \frac{1}{5}$ $y = \frac{3}{5x} + \frac{1}{5}$

5. $m = ^-4$ $b = \frac{3}{4}$ $y = ^-4x + \frac{3}{4}$

6. $m = 0$ $b = \frac{2}{5}$ $y = \frac{2}{5}$

7. $m = \frac{1}{4}$ $b = \frac{2}{3}$ $y = \frac{1}{4x} + \frac{2}{3}$

CD-104316 • © Carson-Dellosa

X- and Y-Intercepts

Writing an Equation of a Line

Slope-Intercept Formula
y = mx + b
m: slope
b: y-intercept containing coordinate points (o, b)

m = 4, passing through points (1, 2)
Using this information, {m = 4, x = 1, y = 2}.
Substitute into y = mx + b to find b.
$2 = (4)(1) + b \longrightarrow 2 = 4 + b$
$2 - 4 = 4 - 4 + b \longrightarrow ^-2 = b$
With the information m = 4, b = ⁻2, write the equation as y = 4x – 2.

Find the equation of the line with the given slope passing through the indicated point (P).

1. m = 3, P (⁻2, ⁻6)
b =
Equation **b = 0, y = 3x**

2. m = 1, P (⁻4, 3)
b =
Equation **b = 7, y = x + 7**

3. m = 0, P (3, 5)
b =
Equation **b = 5, y = 5**

4. m = 3, P (5, 7)
b =
Equation **b = ⁻8, y = 3x – 8**

5. m = ⁻7, P (⁻7, ⁻7)
b =
Equation **b = ⁻56, y = ⁻7x – 56**

6. m = 4, P (2, ⁻6)
b =
Equation **b = ⁻14, y = 4x – 14**

7. m = 4, P (2, 4)
b =
Equation **b = ⁻4, y = 4x – 4**

8. m = ⁻5, P (6, ⁻1)
b =
Equation **b = 29, y = ⁻5x + 29**

9. m = 2, P (⁻1, 1)
b =
Equation **b = 3, y = 2x + 3**

10. m = 2, P (⁻1, ⁻6)
b =
Equation **b = ⁻4, y = 2x – 4**

11. m = ⁻2, P (4, 5)
b =
Equation **b = 13, y = ⁻2x + 13**

12. m = ⁻6, P (2, 6)
b =
Equation **b = 18, y = ⁻6x + 18**

CD-104316 • © Carson-Dellosa

X- and Y-Intercepts

Graphing Linear Inequalities

Graph: y > 2x + 3

1. Graph the line y = 2x + 3. $m = \frac{2}{1}$ $b = 3$

2. If > or <, connect points with dotted line

3. If ≥ or ≤, connect points with solid line
The coordinate plane is now divided into 2 regions.

4. Test any (x, y) on each side of the line that divides the plane into the 2 regions. Test (x, y) in the original inequality.

Test point A.
Test point B.

y > 2x + 3
Test point A (⁻1, 4).
Is 4 > 2 (⁻1) + 3?
4 > ⁻2 + 3
4 > 1 → true
(Shade this region)
Test point A.

y > 2x + 3
Test point B (0, 0).
Is 0 > (0) + 3?
0 > 0 + 3
0 > 3 → false
(Do not shade this region)
Test point B.

Graph the solution set.

1. $x + 4y > 8$ $y > ^-\frac{1}{4}x + 2$

2. $^-2x + 2y > 10$ $y > x + 5$

CD-104316 • © Carson-Dellosa

CD-104316 • © Carson-Dellosa

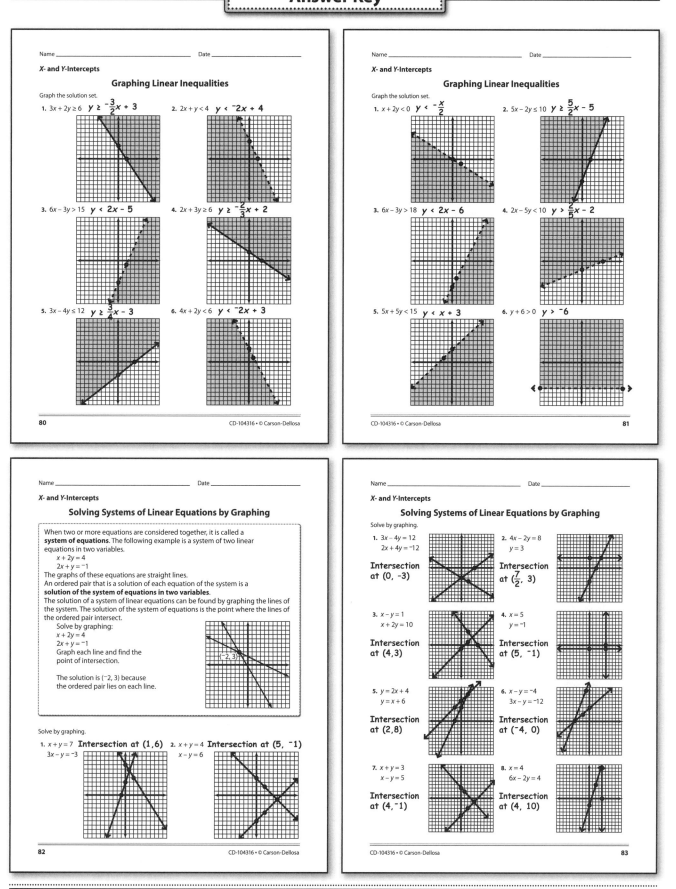

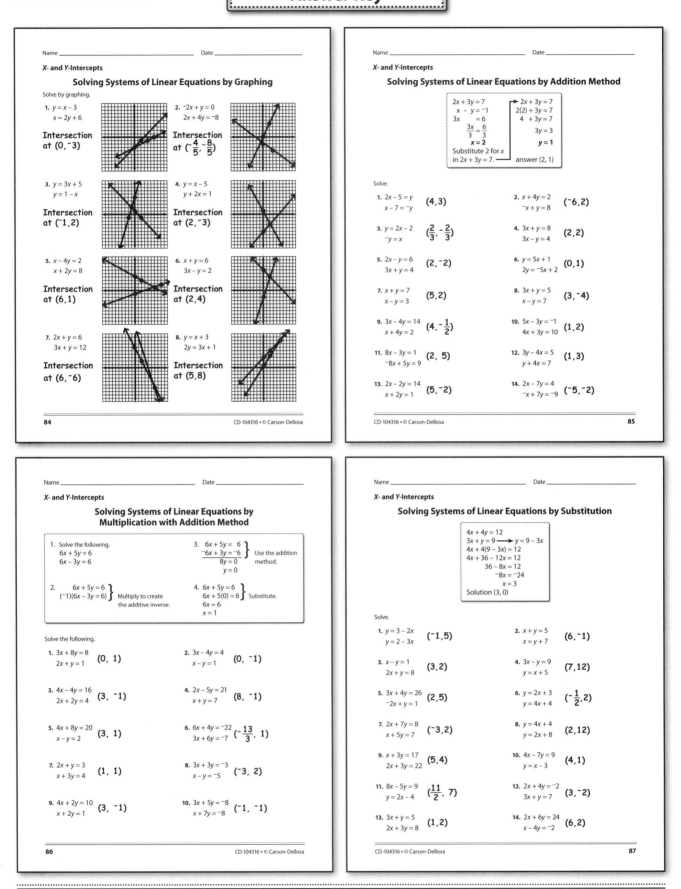

Name _____ Date _____

X- and *Y*-Intercepts

Solving Systems of Linear Equations by Graphing

Solve by graphing.

1. $y = x - 3$
   $x = 2y + 6$

   Intersection at $(0, ^-3)$

2. $^-2x + y = 0$
   $2x + 4y = ^-8$

   Intersection at $(^-\frac{4}{5}, ^-\frac{8}{5})$

3. $y = 3x + 5$
   $y = 1 - x$

   Intersection at $(^-1, 2)$

4. $y = x - 5$
   $y + 2x = 1$

   Intersection at $(2, ^-3)$

5. $x - 4y = 2$
   $x + 2y = 8$

   Intersection at $(6, 1)$

6. $x + y = 6$
   $3x - y = 2$

   Intersection at $(2, 4)$

7. $2x + y = 6$
   $3x + y = 12$

   Intersection at $(6, ^-6)$

8. $y = x + 3$
   $2y = 3x + 1$

   Intersection at $(5, 8)$

84   CD-104316 • © Carson-Dellosa

Name _____ Date _____

X- and *Y*-Intercepts

Solving Systems of Linear Equations by Addition Method

$2x + 3y = 7$ $2x + 3y = 7$
$\underline{x - y = ^-1}$ $2(2) + 3y = 7$
$3x = 6$ $4 + 3y = 7$
$\dfrac{3x}{3} = \dfrac{6}{3}$ $3y = 3$
$\mathbf{x = 2}$ $\mathbf{y = 1}$
Substitute 2 for *x*
in $2x + 3y = 7$.   answer (2, 1)

Solve.

1. $2x - 5 = y$
   $x - 7 = ^-y$ (4, 3)

2. $x + 4y = 2$
   $^-x + y = 8$ $(^-6, 2)$

3. $y = 2x - 2$
   $^-y = x$ $(\frac{2}{3}, -\frac{2}{3})$

4. $3x + y = 8$
   $3x - y = 4$ (2, 2)

5. $2x - y = 6$
   $3x + y = 4$ $(2, ^-2)$

6. $y = 5x + 1$
   $2y = ^-5x + 2$ (0, 1)

7. $x + y = 7$
   $x - y = 3$ (5, 2)

8. $3x + y = 5$
   $x - y = 7$ $(3, ^-4)$

9. $3x - 4y = 14$
   $x + 4y = 2$ $(4, -\frac{1}{2})$

10. $5x - 3y = ^-1$
    $4x + 3y = 10$ (1, 2)

11. $8x - 3y = 1$
    $^-8x + 5y = 9$ (2, 5)

12. $3y - 4x = 5$
    $y + 4x = 7$ (1, 3)

13. $2x - 2y = 14$
    $x + 2y = 1$ $(5, ^-2)$

14. $2x - 7y = 4$
    $^-x + 7y = ^-9$ $(^-5, ^-2)$

CD-104316 • © Carson-Dellosa   85

Name _____ Date _____

X- and *Y*-Intercepts

Solving Systems of Linear Equations by Multiplication with Addition Method

1. Solve the following.
   $6x + 5y = 6$
   $6x - 3y = 6$

2. $6x + 5y = 6$
   $(^-1)(6x - 3y = 6)$ } Multiply to create the additive inverse.

3. $6x + 5y = 6$
   $\underline{^-6x + 3y = ^-6}$ } Use the addition method.
   $8y = 0$
   $y = 0$

4. $6x + 5y = 6$
   $6x + 5(0) = 6$ } Substitute.
   $6x = 6$
   $x = 1$

Solve the following.

1. $3x + 8y = 8$
   $2x + y = 1$ (0, 1)

2. $3x - 4y = 4$
   $x - y = 1$ $(0, ^-1)$

3. $4x - 4y = 16$
   $2x + 2y = 4$ $(3, ^-1)$

4. $2x - 5y = 21$
   $x + y = 7$ $(8, ^-1)$

5. $4x + 8y = 20$
   $x - y = 2$ (3, 1)

6. $6x + 4y = ^-22$
   $3x + 6y = ^-7$ $(^-\frac{13}{3}, 1)$

7. $2x + y = 3$
   $x + 3y = 4$ (1, 1)

8. $3x + 3y = ^-3$
   $x - y = ^-5$ $(^-3, 2)$

9. $4x + 2y = 10$
   $x + 2y = 1$ $(3, ^-1)$

10. $3x + 5y = ^-8$
    $x + 7y = ^-8$ $(^-1, ^-1)$

86   CD-104316 • © Carson-Dellosa

Name _____ Date _____

X- and *Y*-Intercepts

Solving Systems of Linear Equations by Substitution

$4x + 4y = 12$
$3x + y = 9 \longrightarrow y = 9 - 3x$
$4x + 4(9 - 3x) = 12$
$4x + 36 - 12x = 12$
$36 - 8x = 12$
$^-8x = ^-24$
$x = 3$
Solution (3, 0)

Solve.

1. $y = 3 - 2x$
   $y = 2 - 3x$ $(^-1, 5)$

2. $x + y = 5$
   $x = y + 7$ $(6, ^-1)$

3. $x - y = 1$
   $2x + y = 8$ (3, 2)

4. $3x - y = 9$
   $y = x + 5$ (7, 12)

5. $3x + 4y = 26$
   $^-2x + y = 1$ (2, 5)

6. $y = 2x + 3$
   $y = 4x + 4$ $(^-\frac{1}{2}, 2)$

7. $2x + 7y = 8$
   $x + 5y = 7$ $(^-3, 2)$

8. $y = 4x + 4$
   $y = 2x + 8$ (2, 12)

9. $x + 3y = 17$
   $2x + 3y = 22$ (5, 4)

10. $4x - 7y = 9$
    $y = x - 3$ (4, 1)

11. $8x - 5y = 9$
    $y = 2x - 4$ $(\frac{11}{2}, 7)$

12. $2x + 4y = ^-2$
    $3x + y = 7$ $(3, ^-2)$

13. $3x + y = 5$
    $2x + 3y = 8$ (1, 2)

14. $2x + 6y = 24$
    $x - 4y = ^-2$ (6, 2)

CD-104316 • © Carson-Dellosa   87

Name _____ Date _____

Radicals

Simplifying Radicals

$$\sqrt{49x^4y^8} = 7\sqrt{x^4y^8} = 7x^2y^4$$

Simplify.

1. $\sqrt{x^2y^{10}} =$ **xy^5**

2. $\sqrt{27x^8} =$ **$3x^4\sqrt{3}$**

3. $\sqrt{x^{16}} =$ **x^8**

4. $\sqrt{125b^{15}} =$ **$5b^7\sqrt{5b}$**

5. $\sqrt{x^{14}y^6} =$ **x^7y^3**

6. $\sqrt{169y^{12}} =$ **$13y^6$**

7. $\sqrt{16x^4} =$ **$4x^2$**

8. $\sqrt{8x^3} =$ **$2x\sqrt{2x}$**

9. $\sqrt{81x^6} =$ **$9x^3$**

10. $\sqrt{25x^6} =$ **$5x^3$**

11. $\sqrt{x^9y^9} =$ **$x^4y^4\sqrt{xy}$**

12. $\sqrt{a^{12}} =$ **a^6**

13. $\sqrt{9a^4b^8} =$ **$3a^2b^4$**

14. $\sqrt{54x^8} =$ **$3x^4\sqrt{6}$**

15. $\sqrt{49x^4y^2} =$ **$7x^2y$**

16. $\sqrt{x^8} =$ **x^4**

17. $\sqrt{8x^9} =$ **$2x^4\sqrt{2x}$**

18. $\sqrt{81x^9y^{12}} =$ **$9x^4y^6\sqrt{x}$**

19. $\sqrt{8x^4} =$ **$2x^2\sqrt{2}$**

20. $\sqrt{x^3y^9} =$ **$xy^4\sqrt{xy}$**

Name _____ Date _____

Radicals

Simplifying Radicals

$$\sqrt{64x^2y^4} = 8\sqrt{x^2y^4} = 8xy^2$$

Simplify.

1. $\sqrt{81x^6} =$ **$9x^3$**

2. $\sqrt{6x^2} =$ **$x\sqrt{6}$**

3. $\sqrt{9x^3} =$ **$3x\sqrt{x}$**

4. $\sqrt{12y^5} =$ **$2y^2\sqrt{3y}$**

5. $\sqrt{9x^4} =$ **$3x^2$**

6. $\sqrt{81x^6} =$ **$9x^3$**

7. $\sqrt{12x^2y^4} =$ **$2xy^2\sqrt{3}$**

8. $\sqrt{6x^9} =$ **$x^4\sqrt{6x}$**

9. $\sqrt{21x^2} =$ **$x\sqrt{21}$**

10. $\sqrt{x^3} =$ **$x\sqrt{x}$**

11. $\sqrt{4x^5y^2} =$ **$2x^2y\sqrt{x}$**

12. $\sqrt{64a^3b^6} =$ **$8ab^3\sqrt{a}$**

13. $\sqrt{4x^7} =$ **$2x^3\sqrt{x}$**

14. $\sqrt{9x^5y^{16}} =$ **$3x^2y^8\sqrt{x}$**

15. $\sqrt{18x^3y^4} =$ **$3xy^2\sqrt{2x}$**

16. $\sqrt{9x^3y^4} =$ **$3xy^2\sqrt{x}$**

17. $\sqrt{12x^4y^8} =$ **$2x^2y^4\sqrt{3}$**

18. $\sqrt{8x^4} =$ **$2x^2\sqrt{2}$**

19. $\sqrt{27x^7} =$ **$3x^3\sqrt{3x}$**

20. $\sqrt{9x^6} =$ **$3x^3$**

Name _____ Date _____

Radicals

Multiplying Radicals

$$\sqrt{3a} \cdot \sqrt{4a} = \sqrt{12a^2} = \sqrt{3} \cdot 4 \cdot a^2 = 2a\sqrt{3}$$

Simplify.

1. $\sqrt{x^2y^4} \cdot 2\sqrt{xy} =$ **$2xy^2\sqrt{xy}$**

2. $\sqrt{9} \cdot \sqrt{32} =$ **$12\sqrt{2}$**

3. $3\sqrt{5} \cdot 2\sqrt{4} =$ **$12\sqrt{5}$**

4. $4\sqrt{9x^3} \cdot 3\sqrt{4x} =$ **$72x^2$**

5. $2\sqrt{4x^3y} \cdot y\sqrt{x^5y^7} =$ **$4x^4y^5$**

6. $x\sqrt{5x^3y} \cdot x\sqrt{5x^5y} =$ **$5x^4y\sqrt{x}$**

7. $2\sqrt{9x^2} \cdot 2\sqrt{4x^2} =$ **$24x^2$**

8. $6\sqrt{9xy} \cdot 4\sqrt{2xy} =$ **$72xy\sqrt{2}$**

9. $2\sqrt{4x^3y} \cdot 3\sqrt{3a^2b^2} =$ **$12abx\sqrt{3xy}$**

10. $5\sqrt{2x^6y} \cdot 3\sqrt{3x^3y^5} =$ **$15x^4y^3\sqrt{6x}$**

11. $4\sqrt{8a^6b} \cdot 4\sqrt{8a^4b^4} =$ **$128a^5b^2\sqrt{b}$**

12. $3\sqrt{2x^3} \cdot 3\sqrt{3x^3y^2} =$ **$9x^2y\sqrt{6x}$**

13. $5\sqrt{4a} \cdot 2\sqrt{6a} =$ **$20a\sqrt{6}$**

14. $x\sqrt{3x} \cdot x\sqrt{3x^3} =$ **$3x^4$**

15. $\sqrt{2x^4} \cdot \sqrt{10x^3y^2} =$ **$2x^3y\sqrt{5}$**

16. $3\sqrt{4x^3y} \cdot 4\sqrt{5x^5y^7} =$ **$24x^4y^4\sqrt{5}$**

17. $x\sqrt{81} \cdot y\sqrt{36} =$ **$54xy$**

18. $4\sqrt{3x} \cdot 4\sqrt{4x} =$ **$32x\sqrt{3}$**

19. $3\sqrt{8a} \cdot 8\sqrt{3a^3} =$ **$48a^2\sqrt{6}$**

20. $2\sqrt{2a^6} \cdot 5\sqrt{3a^3b^5} =$ **$10a^4b^2\sqrt{6ab}$**

Name _____ Date _____

Radicals

Dividing Radicals

$$\sqrt{\frac{18}{2}} = \sqrt{9} = 3 \qquad \sqrt{\frac{9}{25}} = \frac{\sqrt{9}}{\sqrt{25}} = \frac{3}{5}$$

Simplify.

1. $\sqrt{\frac{36}{9}} =$ **2**

2. $\sqrt{\frac{27x}{3x}} =$ **3**

3. $\sqrt{\frac{x^2}{25}} =$ **$\frac{x}{5}$**

4. $\sqrt{\frac{8x^3}{2x}} =$ **$2x$**

5. $\sqrt{\frac{18x^3}{2x}} =$ **$3x$**

6. $\sqrt{\frac{9}{64}} =$ **$\frac{3}{8}$**

7. $\sqrt{\frac{27x^2}{3}} =$ **$3x$**

8. $\sqrt{\frac{50x^2}{2}} =$ **$5x$**

9. $\sqrt{\frac{49x^2}{25x^3}} =$ **$\frac{7}{5\sqrt{x}}$**

10. $\sqrt{\frac{12x^2}{60}} =$ **$\frac{x}{\sqrt{5}}$**

11. $\sqrt{\frac{4x^3y}{4xy^3}} =$ **$\frac{x}{y}$**

12. $\sqrt{\frac{3x^4y^5}{x^3y^2}} =$ **$y\sqrt{3xy}$**

13. $\sqrt{\frac{2x^2}{18x^4}} =$ **$\frac{1}{3x}$**

14. $\sqrt{\frac{3x^7}{108y^2}} =$ **$\frac{x^3\sqrt{x}}{6y}$**

Name _____ Date _____

Radicals

Adding and Subtracting Radical Expressions

$2\sqrt{y}$	$\sqrt{y}$	$\sqrt{y}$	$\sqrt{y}$	$\sqrt{4x}$	$\sqrt{x}$	$\sqrt{x}$	$\sqrt{x}$	$\sqrt{x}$

$+3 \quad + \quad = 6 \qquad +3 \quad = 2 \quad +3 \quad = 5$

Simplify.

1. $3\sqrt{x^3} - 4\sqrt{x^3} = \ ^-x\sqrt{x}$

2. $3\sqrt{2y} + 2\sqrt{2y} = \mathbf{5\sqrt{2y}}$

3. $2\sqrt{y} - 4\sqrt{y} = \ ^-\mathbf{2\sqrt{y}}$

4. $3y\sqrt{2y} - y\sqrt{2y} = \mathbf{2y\sqrt{2y}}$

5. $x\sqrt{27} + x\sqrt{12} = \mathbf{5x\sqrt{3}}$

6. $3\sqrt{6x} + 5\sqrt{6x} = \mathbf{8\sqrt{6x}}$

7. $4\sqrt{2x^3} + 3\sqrt{2x^3} = \mathbf{7x\sqrt{2x}}$

8. $2\sqrt{50} - 4\sqrt{8} - 3\sqrt{72} = \ ^-\mathbf{16\sqrt{2}}$

9. $4\sqrt{y^3} - 2\sqrt{y^3} = \mathbf{2y\sqrt{y}}$

10. $3\sqrt{x^3} + 3\sqrt{x^2} = \mathbf{3x + 3x\sqrt{x}}$

11. $y\sqrt{y^4} - 2y\sqrt{y^4} = \ ^-\mathbf{y^3}$

12. $x\sqrt{6x} + x\sqrt{24x} = \mathbf{3x\sqrt{6x}}$

13. $4x\sqrt{x^3} + 2x\sqrt{x^3} = \mathbf{6x^2\sqrt{x}}$

14. $5\sqrt{24y} + \sqrt{54y} = \mathbf{13\sqrt{6y}}$

15. $4\sqrt{x} - 2\sqrt{x} - 3\sqrt{x} + 5\sqrt{x} = \mathbf{4\sqrt{x}}$

16. $3\sqrt{4x^2y} - 8y\sqrt{y} = \mathbf{(6x - 8y)\sqrt{y}}$

17. $3\sqrt{9x^2y^2} + 2\sqrt{9x^2y^2} = \mathbf{15xy}$

18. $6\sqrt{6y} + 7\sqrt{6y} + 2\sqrt{6y} = \mathbf{15\sqrt{6y}}$

19. $3x\sqrt{4x^3y^2} - 5\sqrt{x^3y^2} = \mathbf{x(6xy - 5y)\sqrt{x}}$

20. $2\sqrt{4x} + 3\sqrt{2x} - 4\sqrt{2x} + 4\sqrt{4x} = \mathbf{12\sqrt{x} - \sqrt{2x}}$

Name _____ Date _____

Factoring

Solving Equations by Taking Square Roots

$$x^2 = 49$$
$$\sqrt{x^2} = \sqrt{49}$$
$$x = \pm 7$$

The solutions are 7 and ⁻7.

Solve by taking square roots.

1. $x^2 = 9 \quad x = \mathbf{\pm 3}$

2. $x^2 - 81 = 0 \quad x = \mathbf{\pm 9}$

3. $x^2 = 144 \quad x = \mathbf{\pm 12}$

4. $x^2 = 100 \quad x = \mathbf{\pm 10}$

5. $a^2 = 196 \quad x = \mathbf{\pm 14}$

6. $x^2 - 49 = 0 \quad x = \mathbf{\pm 7}$

7. $5x^2 - 125 = 0 \quad x = \mathbf{\pm 5}$

8. $x^2 - 121 = 0 \quad x = \mathbf{\pm 11}$

9. $x^2 - 64 = 0 \quad x = \mathbf{\pm 8}$

10. $x^2 - 361 = 0 \quad x = \mathbf{\pm 19}$

11. $x^2 + 81 = 162 \quad x = \mathbf{\pm 9}$

12. $3x^2 - 432 = 0 \quad x = \mathbf{\pm 12}$

13. $3x^2 - 108 = 0 \quad x = \mathbf{\pm 6}$

14. $a^2 - 169 = 0 \quad x = \mathbf{\pm 13}$

15. $2x^2 - 128 = 0 \quad x = \mathbf{\pm 8}$

16. $2a^2 - 242 = 0 \quad x = \mathbf{\pm 11}$

17. $x^2 - 225 = 0 \quad x = \mathbf{\pm 15}$

18. $3x^2 - 147 = 0 \quad x = \mathbf{\pm 7}$

19. $x^2 - 25 = 0 \quad x = \mathbf{\pm 5}$

20. $4x^2 - 16 = 0 \quad x = \mathbf{\pm 2}$

Name _____ Date _____

Factoring

Solving Quadratic Equations by Factoring

$$x^2 - 8x = ^-16 \qquad x - 4 = 0$$
$$x^2 - 8x + 16 = 0 \qquad x = 4$$
$$(x - 4)(x - 4) = 0 \qquad \text{The solution is 4.}$$

Solve by factoring.

1. $y^2 + 9y = 0$
$\mathbf{y(y + 9) = 0, \{^-9, 0\}}$

2. $x - 16 = x(x - 7)$
$\mathbf{(x - 4)(x - 4) = 0, \{4\}}$

3. $x - 6 = x(x - 4)$
$\mathbf{(x - 3)(x - 2) = 0, \{2,3\}}$

4. $x^2 + 7x = 0$
$\mathbf{x(x + 7) = 0, \{0, ^-7\}}$

5. $x^2 - 4x = 0$
$\mathbf{x(x - 4) = 0, \{0,4\}}$

6. $x + 8 = x(x + 3)$
$\mathbf{(x + 4)(x - 2) = 0, \{^-4,2\}}$

7. $y^2 - y - 6 = 0$
$\mathbf{(y - 3)(y + 2) = 0, \{^-2,3\}}$

8. $a^2 - 36 = 0$
$\mathbf{(a - 6)(a + 6) = 0, \{-6,6\}}$

9. $y^2 + 15 = 8y$
$\mathbf{(y - 3)(y - 5) = 0, \{3,5\}}$

10. $a^2 - 7a = ^-12$
$\mathbf{(a - 3)(a - 4) = 0, \{3,4\}}$

11. $y^2 + 36y = 0$
$\mathbf{y(y + 36) = 0, \{0, ^-36\}}$

12. $3u^2 - 12u - 15 = 0$
$\mathbf{3(u - 5)(u + 1) = 0, \{^-1,5\}}$

13. $y^2 - 8y + 12 = 0$
$\mathbf{(y - 6)(y - 2) = 0, \{2,6\}}$

14. $5a^2 + 25a = 0$
$\mathbf{5a(a + 5) = 0, \{^-5,0\}}$

15. $6x^2 + 18x = 0$
$\mathbf{6x(x + 3) = 0, \{^-3,0\}}$

16. $2x^2 + x = 6$
$\mathbf{(2x - 3)(x + 2) = 0, \{^-2, \frac{3}{2}\}}$

17. $x^2 - 5x - 6 = 0$
$\mathbf{(x - 6)(x + 1) = 0, \{^-1,6\}}$

18. $4x^2 + 16x = 0$
$\mathbf{4x(x + 4) = 0, \{0, ^-4\}}$

19. $3x^2 - 9x = 0$
$\mathbf{3x(x - 3) = 0, \{0,3\}}$

20. $y^2 + 5y - 6 = 0$
$\mathbf{(y + 6)(y - 1) = 0, \{^-6,1\}}$

Name _____ Date _____

Factoring

Solving Quadratic Equations by Factoring

Solve by factoring.

1. $a^2 - 8a = 0$
$\mathbf{a(a - 8) = 0, \{0,8\}}$

2. $x^2 = 3x + 4$
$\mathbf{(x - 4)(x + 1) = 0, \{^-1,4\}}$

3. $4a^2 + 15a - 4 = 0$
$\mathbf{(4a - 1)(a + 4) = 0, \{\frac{1}{4}, ^-4\}}$

4. $x^2 - x - 6 = 0$
$\mathbf{(x - 3)(x + 2) = 0, \{^-2,3\}}$

5. $3x^2 - 13x + 4 = 0$
$\mathbf{(3x - 1)(x - 4) = 0, \{\frac{1}{3},4\}}$

6. $6x^2 = 23x + 18$
$\mathbf{(3x + 2)(2x - 9) = 0, \{^-\frac{2}{3}, \frac{9}{2}\}}$

7. $x^2 + 7x + 12 = 0$
$\mathbf{(x + 4)(x + 3) = 0, \{^-4, ^-3\}}$

8. $x^2 + 5x - 6 = 0$
$\mathbf{(x + 6)(x - 1) = 0, \{^-6,1\}}$

9. $x^2 = 6x + 7$
$\mathbf{(x - 7)(x + 1) = 0, \{^-1,7\}}$

10. $x^2 = 10x - 25$
$\mathbf{(x - 5)(x - 5) = 0, \{5\}}$

11. $x^2 + 3x - 10 = 0$
$\mathbf{(x + 5)(x - 2) = 0, \{^-5,2\}}$

12. $x^2 - 6x + 9 = 0$
$\mathbf{(x - 3)(x - 3) = 0, \{3\}}$

13. $y^2 - 3y + 2 = 0$
$\mathbf{(y - 2)(y - 1) = 0, \{1,2\}}$

14. $2x^2 - 9x + 9 = 0$
$\mathbf{(2x - 3)(x - 3) = 0, \{\frac{3}{2},3\}}$

15. $r^2 - 15r = 16$
$\mathbf{(r - 16)(r + 1) = 0, \{^-1,16\}}$

16. $x^2 + 7x + 10 = 0$
$\mathbf{(x + 2)(x + 5) = 0, \{^-5, ^-2\}}$

17. $3x^2 - 2x - 8 = 0$
$\mathbf{(3x + 4)(x - 2) = 0, \{^-\frac{4}{3},2\}}$

18. $2a^2 + 4a - 6 = 0$
$\mathbf{(2a - 2)(a + 3) = 0, \{^-3,1\}}$

19. $x^2 + 3x - 4 = 0$
$\mathbf{(x + 4)(x - 1) = 0, \{^-4,1\}}$

20. $4a^2 + 9a + 2 = 0$
$\mathbf{(4a + 1)(a + 2) = 0, \{^-2, ^-\frac{1}{4}\}}$

21. $9x^2 = 18x + 0$
$\mathbf{9x(x - 2) = 0, \{0,2\}}$

22. $2x^2 = 9x + 5$
$\mathbf{(2x + 1)(x - 5) = 0, \{^-\frac{1}{2},5\}}$

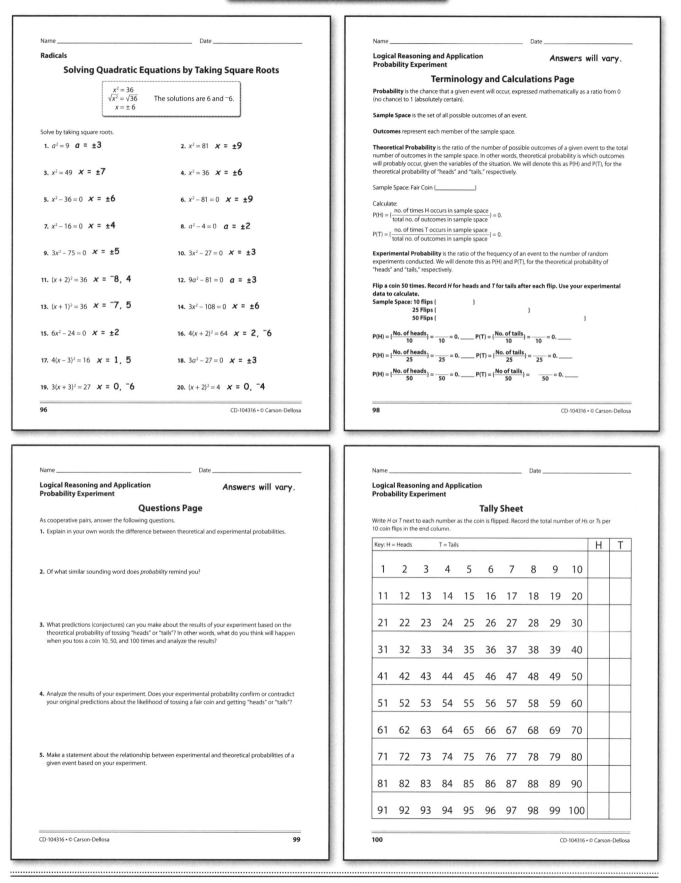

Name _____ Date _____

Radicals

Solving Quadratic Equations by Taking Square Roots

$$x^2 = 36$$
$$\sqrt{x^2} = \sqrt{36}$$ The solutions are 6 and ⁻6.
$$x = \pm 6$$

Solve by taking square roots.

1. $a^2 = 9$ **a = ±3**

2. $x^2 = 81$ **x = ±9**

3. $x^2 = 49$ **x = ±7**

4. $x^2 = 36$ **x = ±6**

5. $x^2 - 36 = 0$ **x = ±6**

6. $x^2 - 81 = 0$ **x = ±9**

7. $x^2 - 16 = 0$ **x = ±4**

8. $a^2 - 4 = 0$ **a = ±2**

9. $3x^2 - 75 = 0$ **x = ±5**

10. $3x^2 - 27 = 0$ **x = ±3**

11. $(x + 2)^2 = 36$ **x = ⁻8, 4**

12. $9a^2 - 81 = 0$ **a = ±3**

13. $(x + 1)^2 = 36$ **x = ⁻7, 5**

14. $3x^2 - 108 = 0$ **x = ±6**

15. $6x^2 - 24 = 0$ **x = ±2**

16. $4(x + 2)^2 = 64$ **x = 2, ⁻6**

17. $4(x - 3)^2 = 16$ **x = 1, 5**

18. $3a^2 - 27 = 0$ **x = ±3**

19. $3(x + 3)^2 = 27$ **x = 0, ⁻6**

20. $(x + 2)^2 = 4$ **x = 0, ⁻4**

96   CD-104316 • © Carson-Dellosa

Name _____ Date _____

Logical Reasoning and Application
Probability Experiment   *Answers will vary.*

Terminology and Calculations Page

Probability is the chance that a given event will occur, expressed mathematically as a ratio from 0 (no chance) to 1 (absolutely certain).

Sample Space is the set of all possible outcomes of an event.

Outcomes represent each member of the sample space.

Theoretical Probability is the ratio of the number of possible outcomes of a given event to the total number of outcomes in the sample space. In other words, theoretical probability is which outcomes will probably occur, given the variables of the situation. We will denote this as P(H) and P(T), for the theoretical probability of "heads" and "tails," respectively.

Sample Space: Fair Coin {_____}

Calculate:

$P(H) = \left\{ \dfrac{\text{no. of times H occurs in sample space}}{\text{total no. of outcomes in sample space}} \right\} = 0.$

$P(T) = \left\{ \dfrac{\text{no. of times T occurs in sample space}}{\text{total no. of outcomes in sample space}} \right\} = 0.$

Experimental Probability is the ratio of the frequency of an event to the number of random experiments conducted. We will denote this as P(H) and P(T), for the theoretical probability of "heads" and "tails," respectively.

Flip a coin 50 times. Record *H* for heads and *T* for tails after each flip. Use your experimental data to calculate.
Sample Space: 10 flips {   }
25 Flips {   }
50 Flips {   }

$P(H) = \left\{ \dfrac{\text{No. of heads}}{10} \right\} = \dfrac{}{10} = 0.\_\_\_$ $P(T) = \left\{ \dfrac{\text{No. of tails}}{10} \right\} = \dfrac{}{10} = 0.\_\_\_$

$P(H) = \left\{ \dfrac{\text{No. of heads}}{25} \right\} = \dfrac{}{25} = 0.\_\_\_$ $P(T) = \left\{ \dfrac{\text{No. of tails}}{25} \right\} = \dfrac{}{25} = 0.\_\_\_$

$P(H) = \left\{ \dfrac{\text{No. of heads}}{50} \right\} = \dfrac{}{50} = 0.\_\_\_$ $P(T) = \left\{ \dfrac{\text{No of tails}}{50} \right\} = \dfrac{}{50} = 0.\_\_\_$

98   CD-104316 • © Carson-Dellosa

Name _____ Date _____

Logical Reasoning and Application
Probability Experiment   *Answers will vary.*

Questions Page

As cooperative pairs, answer the following questions.

1. Explain in your own words the difference between theoretical and experimental probabilities.

2. Of what similar sounding word does *probability* remind you?

3. What predictions (conjectures) can you make about the results of your experiment based on the theoretical probability of tossing "heads" or "tails"? In other words, what do you think will happen when you toss a coin 10, 50, and 100 times and analyze the results?

4. Analyze the results of your experiment. Does your experimental probability confirm or contradict your original predictions about the likelihood of tossing a fair coin and getting "heads" or "tails"?

5. Make a statement about the relationship between experimental and theoretical probabilities of a given event based on your experiment.

CD-104316 • © Carson-Dellosa   99

Name _____ Date _____

Logical Reasoning and Application
Probability Experiment

Tally Sheet

Write *H* or *T* next to each number as the coin is flipped. Record the total number of *H*s or *T*s per 10 coin flips in the end column.

Key: H = Heads	T = Tails									H	T
1	2	3	4	5	6	7	8	9	10		
11	12	13	14	15	16	17	18	19	20		
21	22	23	24	25	26	27	28	29	30		
31	32	33	34	35	36	37	38	39	40		
41	42	43	44	45	46	47	48	49	50		
51	52	53	54	55	56	57	58	59	60		
61	62	63	64	65	66	67	68	69	70		
71	72	73	74	75	76	77	78	79	80		
81	82	83	84	85	86	87	88	89	90		
91	92	93	94	95	96	97	98	99	100		

100   CD-104316 • © Carson-Dellosa

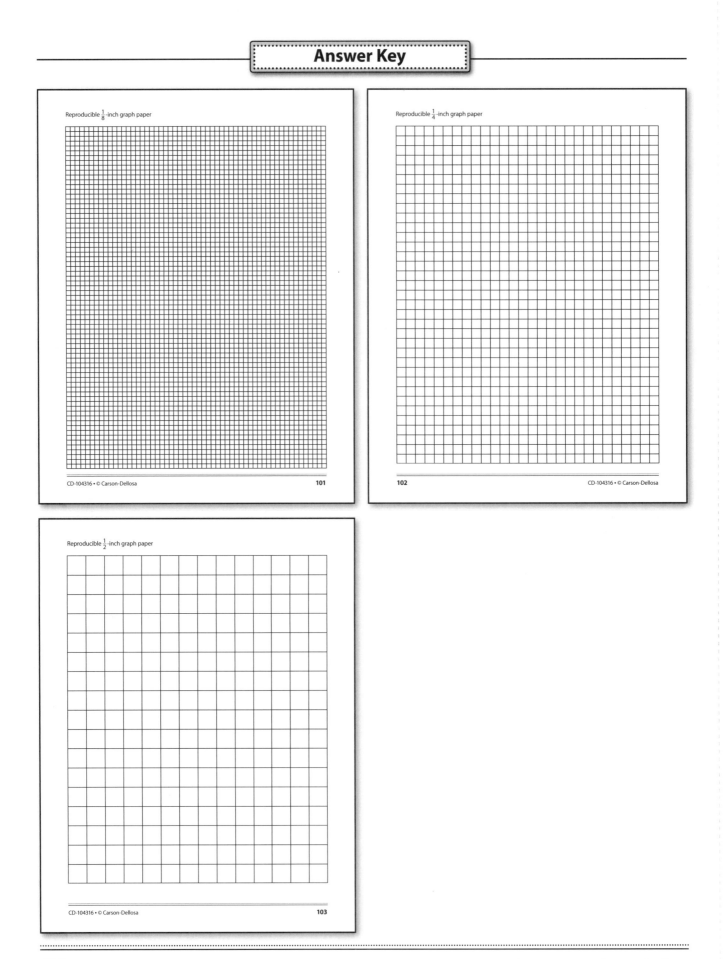

Reproducible $\frac{1}{8}$-inch graph paper

CD-104316 • © Carson-Dellosa   **101**

Reproducible $\frac{1}{4}$-inch graph paper

102   CD-104316 • © Carson-Dellosa

Reproducible $\frac{1}{2}$-inch graph paper

CD-104316 • © Carson-Dellosa   **103**

Congratulations!

_____

receives this award for

_____

Signed _____

Date _____

© Carson–Dellosa

$$\frac{x}{2} = 24$$

$$x - 4 = {}^-3$$

$$4 - x = 6$$

$$3x - 3 = 12$$

$$3x \div 3 = 12$$

$$-7x + {}^-4 = 17$$

$$x + 9 = {}^-12$$

$$x - 5 = {}^-3$$

$$x - 3 = {}^-6$$

$$\frac{x}{3} = {}^-6$$

$$x - 4 = 6$$

$$x + 4 = {}^-10$$

$$x + 6 = {}^-6$$

$$5x - 17 = 8$$

$$x + 5 = {}^-7$$

$$-4x = 36$$

© CD

$x = 48$ $x = 12$ $x = -3$ $x = -12$

$x = 1$ $x = -3$ $x = -18$ $x = 5$

$x = -2$ $x = -21$ $x = 10$ $x = -12$

$x = 5$ $x = 2$ $x = -14$ $x = -9$

$$\left(\frac{x^3}{y^2}\right)^4$$

$$\frac{18x^3}{3x}$$

$$x^3 \cdot x \cdot x \cdot x^2$$

$$x^4 \cdot x^4 \cdot x^4$$

© CD

$$(x^3y^2)^3$$

$$\frac{x^{12}}{x^3}$$

$$7x^{-6}$$

$$(-3)^{-2}$$

© CD

$$\left(\frac{3}{4}\right)^{-2}$$

$$\frac{(x^6 \cdot x^4)}{x^2}$$

$$(6x^{-2})^2$$

$$(-7x^3)^{-2}$$

© CD

$$(3xy)^{-1}$$

$$(3x^2)(4x^3)$$

$$(2x^3)^3$$

$$(3x^2y^2)^3$$

© CD

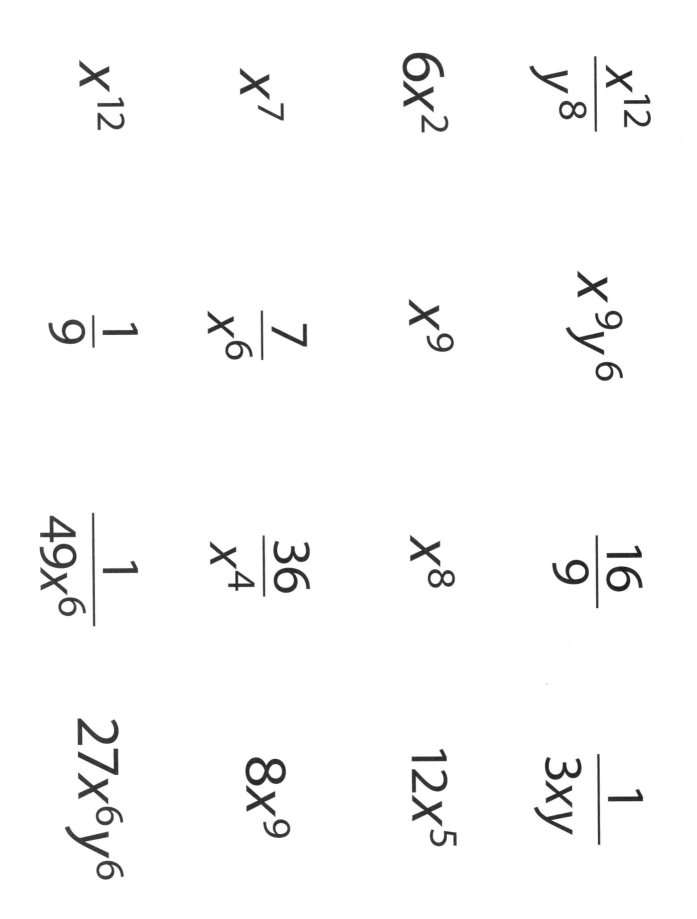

$$\frac{x^{12}}{y^8}$$

$$x^9 y^6$$

$$\frac{16}{9}$$

$$\frac{1}{3xy}$$

$$6x^2$$

$$x^9$$

$$x^8$$

$$12x^5$$

$$x^7$$

$$\frac{7}{x^6}$$

$$\frac{36}{x^4}$$

$$8x^9$$

$$x^{12}$$

$$\frac{1}{9}$$

$$\frac{1}{49x^6}$$

$$27x^6 y^6$$

$(-2)^3$

$x^3 \cdot x^2 \cdot x^3$

$(5x^3)^2$

$x^3 \cdot x^{-7}$

$\dfrac{x^6}{x^3}$

$(x^3)^3$

$(x^8)^2$

$(4x)^{-2}$

$x^2 \cdot x^4$

$\left(\dfrac{3}{4}\right)^{-2}$

$x^3 \cdot x^3$

$3x^{-3}$

2^{-3}

$5x^{-3}$

$(x^6)^3$

$x^6 \cdot x^{-3}$

© CD

-8

x^8

$\dfrac{1}{x^4}$

$25x^6$

x^3

x^9

x^{16}

$\dfrac{1}{16x^2}$

x^6

$\dfrac{16}{9}$

x^6

$\dfrac{3}{x^3}$

x^3

x^{18}

$\dfrac{5}{x^3}$

$\dfrac{1}{8}$

© CD

Factor.

$$36x^2 + 6x + 12$$

© CD

Factor.

$$81 - x^2$$

© CD

Factor.

$$25x^2 - y^2$$

© CD

Factor.

$$(x^2 + 6x + 9)$$

© CD

Factor.

$$2(4 - y)$$

© CD

Factor.

$$9x^2 - 16$$

© CD

Factor.

$$36x^2 + 49y^2$$

© CD

Factor.

$$x^2 + 5x + 6$$

© CD

Factor.

$$3x + 4x^2$$

© CD

Factor.

$$x^2 - 4$$

© CD

Factor.

$$36x^2 - 81$$

© CD

Factor.

$$5x^2 - 35$$

© CD

Factor.

$$6x + 12y$$

© CD

Factor.

$$4x^2 + 64$$

© CD

Factor.

$$x^2 - 9$$

© CD

Factor.

$$3x^2 - 36$$

© CD

$6(6x^2 + x + 2)$ $2(4 - y)$ $x(3 + 4x)$ $6(x + 2y)$

$(9 - x)(9 + x)$ $(3x - 4)(3x + 4)$ $(x - 2)(x + 2)$ $4(x^2 + 16)$

$(5x - y)(5x + y)$ $(6x + 7y)(6x - 7y)$ $9(2x - 3)(2x + 3)$ $(x - 3)(x + 3)$

$(x + 3)(x + 3)$ $(x + 3)(x + 2)$ $5(x^2 - 7)$ $3(x^2 - 12)$

© CD

Factor.

$$x^2 + 9x + 14$$

Factor.

$$x^2 + 10x + 16$$

Factor.

$$x^2 - 8x + 15$$

Factor.

$$x^2 - 12x + 36$$

© CD

Factor.

$$x^2 - 10x + 24$$

Factor.

$$x^2 + 11x + 28$$

Factor.

$$x^2 - 5x - 6$$

Factor.

$$x^2 - x - 72$$

© CD

Factor.

$$x^2 - 3x - 10$$

Factor.

$$x^2 - 2x - 8$$

Factor.

$$x^2 + 4x - 21$$

Factor.

$$x^2 + 2x - 15$$

© CD

Factor.

$$x^2 + 2x - 24$$

Factor.

$$x^2 - 13x - 48$$

Factor.

$$3x^4 - 243$$

Factor.

$$2x^2 - 4x - 48$$

© CD

$(x - 6)(x - 6) \quad (x - 3)(x - 5) \quad (x + 8)(x + 2) \quad (x + 7)(x + 2)$

$(x - 9)(x + 8) \quad (x - 6)(x + 1) \quad (x + 7)(x + 4) \quad (x - 6)(x - 4)$

$(x + 5)(x - 3) \quad (x + 7)(x - 3) \quad (x - 4)(x + 2) \quad (x - 5)(x + 2)$

$2(x - 6)(x + 4) \quad (x - 16)(x + 3) \quad (x + 6)(x - 4)$

$\qquad\qquad 3(x + 3)(x - 3)$

$\qquad\qquad (x^2 + 9)$